Repaid

An Artist's Guide to Student Loans
& Financial Self-Advocacy

By Matthew Carlson
Artists Financial Support Group

"He looks the whole world in the face,
for he owes not any man."

Henry Wadsworth Longfellow

Table of Contents

Introduction

Where Do I Start?

You might be skeptical. If you are in your last year of an undergraduate or graduate training program and the faculty made you buy this book, you might think: "Why do I need to learn about student loans and budgeting? I'll never need a day job, success will come early, and everything will fall into place." Or you might be desperate. If you are a working artist several years out of school and are quickly browsing through these pages, you might think: "What can this book possibly tell me that will stop the calls from debt collection agencies? I can't afford to be an artist, success will never come, and everything is falling apart."

Young artists are often given contradictory advice. Parents will warn you about the impossible financial struggle ahead, because they want to spare you the stress of being a "starving artist." Teachers will tell you that talent always rises to the top, because they want to encourage you and your art. Well, let's clear this up right away: neither advice is true. The financial life of an artist is erratic and frustrating, but not impossible. And the most talented person doesn't always get the job. The truth is not necessarily easy to hear. We plan on telling you the truth, as best we can.

The Artists Financial Support Group (AFSG) is an organization of working artists who strongly believe that a financially savvy artist is a better artist. We promote **financial self-advocacy**, an assertion of self-determination and personal responsibility in your financial life. The knowledge we will share with you is practical, not theoretical; it comes from actually living the life of an artist. We attempt to confront the unique financial concerns of artists with innovative and sensible solutions. Since 2011, we have led workshops at the NYU Graduate Acting Program, Yale School of Drama, Juilliard, the Actors Fund, and the SAG Foundation. The goal of this book is simple: to share everything we wished someone had told us before we finished school, tangible information about the financial lives of working artists. Nevertheless, you should use financial self-advocacy to research further information on your own. The topics covered in this book have a tendency to change rapidly, and it is your responsibility to learn the details and make informed decisions. We hope to empower you to take personal responsibility for your financial life. We can give advice, but the decisions are ultimately yours.

A major focus of this book is student loans. If you are a current student or recent graduate, you've probably paid a considerable amount of money for a degree in the arts. Unfortunately, we may have reached the point where the cost of an arts education outweighs its value. According to the *New York Times*, total student loan debt in America reached $1.4 trillion in 2017, far surpassing even national credit card debt. When The College Board released its 2016 report on Trends in College Pricing, it again confirmed that tuition continues to increase at a rate significantly higher than the growth in either inflation or the average household income. Yet despite this increase in tuition and student debt, data from the Department of Education reflects a marked increase of students graduating with degrees in the visual and performing arts during the last few decades. The rising price of education, combined with a surplus of aspiring artists, leaves graduates with a staggering amount of debt and an extraordinarily competitive job market.

Throughout this book we will use an example of a consolidated student loan for $100,000. This may seem like an unrealistically large number, but graduates of elite artistic training programs will tell you that it is unfortunately quite real. How do you negotiate exorbitant student loan payments on an erratic income? How do you plan to buy a house or have children? Even for successful working artists, student debt can seem insurmountable compared to income. The challenges we face leave young artists feeling isolated, without hope, and perhaps worse, without art.

This is why you should read *Repaid: An Artist's Guide to Student Loans And Financial Self-Advocacy*. The success of an artist requires more than talent and perseverance: it requires a strong education in personal finance. You cannot wait for extraordinary success - the series regular job on television or the sale of your paintings at a New York gallery. Whether you're a writer, painter, dancer, actor, composer, singer, designer, director, or artist of any medium, you are capable of taking control of your finances. With self-discipline, a freelancer's tenacity, and an artist's creativity, a career in the arts is possible. You will repay your loans. But it can't be done without taking ownership of your financial education and responsibility for your financial life.

A brief disclaimer: we are artists, not bankers. Read this advice from your peers and then educate yourself about your specific circumstances. Recognize that you're not alone and that debt is a shared experience. Turn the page and take the next step toward financial self-advocacy.

The Artists Financial Support Group
Freddy Arsenault, Matthew Carlson,
Ben Graney, Timothy Sekk, & Stephen Stocking

Identification

How Do Student Loans Work?

So you've finished school. You're in debt. You've probably received mail already from both the government and your private lenders (if you have them). You know you should do something about it, but it's much easier to ignore them, to put the letters in a pile of things to do later, or to throw them into the trash unopened. Though these might seem like easier ways to deal with your debt, believe us, they're not. Better to be informed and figure out what your options are, learn what loans you have, and start to take action. Let's take a look at what you need to know, and make that pile of envelopes a little less terrifying.

The following information will help you identify which loans you have, what interest has been accruing, and what exactly has been happening while you've been in school. We'll address consolidation in a later section, but for now, let's just explain what it is you are actually looking at when you first open that envelope on your desk. No need to panic, just take a deep breath. We'll walk you through what you need to know.

The Basics About Loans

Even the language of finance is intimidating, especially for artists. Maybe you didn't do so well in high school economics, or maybe it's been a few years. If you don't immediately understand your loan statements, know this: You are not stupid. The convenience of credit allows borrowers to sign without really knowing the details.

However if you know the basics and learn the lingo, you will feel much more in control. Let's take a look at a simple example loan and start to get familiar with what the financial language means. As an example, let's borrow five thousand (hypothetical) dollars from the bank and look at how loans work.

The **principal** of a loan refers to the base amount owed: the initial amount borrowed when you first take out a loan. In our example, the principal is $5,000. An **interest rate** is the fee a bank charges you for borrowing money, calculated as a percentage of the original loan amount. The fee is calculated annually, and therefore is often referred to as an **annual percentage rate** or **APR**. Let's say that we have an APR of 10% for our example loan of $5,000, and that the interest rate is fixed. A **fixed interest rate** is a percentage-based fee that remains the same throughout the life of the loan. So how does it work? The first year you take out the loan, the interest will be:

$5,000 (principal) x 10% (APR) = $500 (interest)

An **adjustable interest rate** is an interest rate that fluctuates over time, usually expressed as a percentage above the **prime rate** (an interest rate set by banks for loans given to the most credit-worthy borrowers). An adjustable rate will be something like "prime plus 3%." As of early 2017, the prime rate is 3.75%, but as recently as 2007 it was as high as 8.25%. When the prime rate fluctuates, so does your APR, which then affects the interest you owe and the payment you need to make.

An **origination fee** is an activation fee, a charge incurred for beginning a transaction with a bank. Think of it like a handling fee from Ticketmaster but a lot more money, calculated as a percentage of the original loan. Let's say that for our example loan of $5,000, the origination fee was 2%. What that means is that the bank will take back $100 of the loan as a fee before you even get the money. When you get a check from the bank, you will only get $4,900.

Capitalization refers to the addition of unpaid interest into the base amount of the loan. What does that mean? Let's say that for the entire first year that you borrowed $5,000 at 10%, you didn't make any payments. Remember, for that year you accrued $500 of interest. Capitalization means the interest is now added to the original principal of $5,000:

$5,000 (principal) + $500 (interest) = $5,500

You now have a loan with a new principal balance of $5,500 after the capitalization of interest.

Does all of this make sense? We're going to move on to the specifics of your student loans, but you will see all these financial terms again (and a few more). If anything is unclear, you'll find an extensive glossary at the end of the book. And if you get confused, hang in there. Everything is not as complicated as it seems.

What Kind of Loans Do I Have?

Most likely, you have federal loans - and perhaps *only* federal loans. You might not realize this yet, but that sentence is very good news. **Federal Loans** are loans offered to you by the government at reduced interest rates. They include Stafford Loans, Perkins Loans, and PLUS Loans, all of which we will discuss in detail. **Private Loans** are loans not guaranteed or subsidized by the government and are offered by private lenders, which may have lower interest rates but may not be as advantageous in terms of repayment plans. In the remainder of this chapter, we will give examples for those of you who have four years of undergraduate loans, and for those of you who have slightly different loans from attending a three-year graduate program. During your time in school, regardless of whether it was an undergraduate or graduate program, you probably took out a combination of federal loans (and perhaps private loans) to the cover the cost. We'll address private loans separately, so the following information refers to your government loans. Let's take a look at how they work:

A **Stafford Loan** is a loan guaranteed by the government, thereby allowing students to borrow at lower interest rates. If you default, the government guarantees that someone will pay for the loan, and you are therefore less of a risk. In case you're playing Trivial Pursuit, it was named after Robert Stafford, a senator from Vermont. The Bipartisan Student Loan Certainty Act of 2013 tied interest rates for all federal student loans to the financial markets. Interest rates will be calculated each June for loans awarded in the subsequent school year. The individual loans will have a fixed interest rate for the life of the loan, but a new rate will be set each year. For 2016-2017, the rates of Stafford Loans were 3.76% for undergraduates and 5.31% for graduates.

Stafford Loans can be both unsubsidized and subsidized. What does that mean, you ask?

A **subsidized loan** is a loan for which *the government will pay the interest* that accrues while the student is in college. The maximum amount of money you can borrow as an undergraduate with a subsidized Stafford Loan is $3,500 for your first year of college, $4,500 for your second year, and

$5,500 for your third and fourth years. (Before July 1, 2012, graduate students were allowed to take out $8,500 per year; now subsidized loans are only offered to undergraduates.) You likely have multiple subsidized Stafford Loans. Because the government has been paying the interest on all of these loans, you would still only owe the original principal amount on each loan when you graduate ($3,500, $4,500 or $5,500 each for undergraduates, or $8,500 each for graduate students prior to 2012).

An **unsubsidized loan** is a loan for which *the government does not pay the interest* while the student is in college. The maximum amount of money you can borrow as an undergraduate with an unsubsidized Stafford Loan depends on whether you are a dependent or independent student. Dependent students, whose parents (or other adults) are helping them through college, can take out $2,000 a year. An independent student, paying for college alone, can take out $6,000 per year in years 1 and 2, and $7,000 per year for years 3 and 4. Graduate students, again, are different: before July 1, 2012 students could take out $12,000 per year in unsubsidized Stafford Loans. Grad students no longer have the option of subsidized loans, so the limit was raised accordingly to $20,500 per year.

Let's now take a look at two examples that should help explain how unsubsidized loans work while you're still in school. The first involves the loans of an independent undergraduate who takes out the full amount of unsubsidized Stafford Loans over the course of four years. The second details a graduate student who similarly takes out the full amount allowed, over the course of a three-year graduate program. For the example, we will assume the loans are disbursed in 2017, meaning that the graduate student no longer has the option of subsidized loans, and takes out $20,500 a year in unsubsidized loans. Let's look at what happens for both, as one unsubsidized Stafford Loan from their first year of school accrues interest at a rate of 3.76% for the undergraduate and 5.31% for the graduate.

EXAMPLE: Unsubsidized Stafford Loan
Independent Undergraduate Student (Freshman-Year Loan)

FRESHMAN-YEAR LOAN
Principal = $6,000 / Interest Rate = 3.76%
Interest Each Year = $6,000 x 3.76% = $225.60
Interest Accrues for 4 Years = $225.60 x 4 = $902.40
Principal at Graduation = $6,000 + $902.40 = $6,902.40

EXAMPLE: Unsubsidized Stafford Loan
Graduate Student (First-Year Loan)

FIRST-YEAR LOAN
Principal = $20,500 / Interest Rate = 5.31%
Interest Each Year = $20,500 x 5.31% = $1,088.55
Interest Accrues for 3 Years = $1,088.55 x 3 = $3,265.65
Principal at Graduation = $20,500 + $3,265.65 = $23,765.65

If you didn't pay off the interest while you were in school, it will capitalize when you graduate. What did that mean again? **Capitalization** refers to the addition of unpaid interest into the **principal**, or base amount of the loan. So for undergraduates, the unsubsidized Stafford Loan you took out freshman year for $6,000 will have gone through four interest cycles, accruing $225.60 each year and causing the loan to grow to $6,902.40 ($6,000 + $902.40 = $6,902.40). For the graduate student, the unsubsidized

Stafford from your first year for $20,500 will have gone through three interest cycles, accruing $1,088.55 each year and causing the loan to grow to $23,765.65 ($20,500 + $3,265.65 = $23,765.65). Does that make sense? If you took out the full amount during the remaining years of your education, each unsubsidized loan will go through similar interest cycles. The growth is more dramatic for the first-year loans because they have gone through more cycles (to put things in perspective, the loan from your final year of school will only go through one interest cycle, as opposed to three or four). Let's see exactly what that looks like for the rest of your unsubsidized Staffords. As an undergraduate, you probably took out three more unsubsidized Stafford Loans, and as a graduate, probably two more loans. The rates will now change each year based on the financial market, but for this example we will continue to use the 2016-2017 rates of 3.76% for undergraduates and 5.31% for grad students.

The loans that you initially signed have grown significantly while you were in school. For an undergrad taking the full amount, you borrowed $26,000 in unsubsidized Stafford Loans, but now owe $28,368.80. For graduate students, you took out $61,500 but you owe $68,031.30 upon graduation. Not exactly what you expected? Feeling a twinge of panic and ready to stop reading? You're experiencing **sticker shock**, the realization that you owe more than you thought.

Sticker shock refers to the moment when you open those envelopes and see exactly how much you owe, as opposed to what you thought you owed. Don't worry, it happened to me too. Take a deep breath.

EXAMPLE: Independent Undergraduate Student

SOPHOMORE-YEAR LOAN
Principal = $6,000 / Interest Rate = 3.76%
Interest Each Year = $6,000 x 3.76% = $225.60
Interest Accrues for 3 Years = $225.60 x 3 = $676.80
Principal at Graduation = $6,000 + $676.80= $6,676.80

JUNIOR-YEAR LOAN
Principal = $7,000 / Interest Rate = 3.76%
Interest Each Year = $7,000 x 3.76% = $263.20
Interest Accrues for 2 Years = $263.20 x 2= $526.40
Principal at Graduation = $7,000 + $526.40= $7,526.40

SENIOR-YEAR LOAN
Principal = $7,000 / Interest Rate = 3.76%
Interest Each Year = $7,000 x 3.76% = $263.20
Interest Accrues for 1 Year = $263.20 x 1 = $263.20
Principal at Graduation = $7,000 + $263.20 = $7,263.20

Thus, four years of unsubsidized undergraduate Stafford Loans might look something like this:

Loan	Principal	Interest	Total
Freshman	$6,000	$902.40	$6,902.40
Sophomore	$6,000	$676.80	$6,676.80
Junior	$7,000	$526.40	$7,526.40
Senior	$7,000	$263.20	$7,263.20

Borrowed: $26,000
Graduation Balance: $28,368.80

EXAMPLE: Graduate Student

SECOND-YEAR LOAN
Principal = $20,500 / Interest Rate = 5.31%
Interest Each Year = $20,500 x 5.31% = $1,088.55
Interest Accrues for 2 Years = $1,088.55 x 2 = $2,177.10
Principal at Graduation = $20,500 + $2,177.10 = $22,677.10

THIRD-YEAR LOAN
Principal = $20,500 / Interest Rate = 5.31 %
Interest Each Year = $20,500 x 5.31% = $1,088.55
Interest Accrues for 1 Year = $1,088.55 x 1 = $1,088.55
Principal at Graduation = $20,500 + $1,088.55 = $21,588.55

Three years of unsubsidized graduate Stafford loans would look something like this:

Loan	Principal	Interest	Total
Year 1	$20,500	$3,265.65	$23,765.65
Year 2	$20,500	$2,177.10	$22,677.10
Year 3	$20,500	$1,088.55	$21,588.55

Borrowed: $61,500
Graduation Balance: $68,031.30

A **Perkins Loan** is given to students with exceptional financial need. The Perkins Loan is a subsidized loan with a fixed interest rate of 5% and a maximum yearly amount of $5,500 for an undergraduate and $8,000 for a graduate student. It works like the subsidized Stafford, but often at a lower interest rate.

PLUS Loans are federal loans available to the parents of undergraduates, as well as to graduate- or professional-degree students. They help defray additional educational expenses not covered by other options. The amount you can borrow is the cost of attendance (determined by the individual school) minus any other financial assistance received. You (or your parents) may have taken out these loans to help cover living expenses while you were at school - things like rent, food, books, and any other education expense (lattes before class, or that MacBook you just had to have). Originally, PLUS was an acronym that stood for Parent Loans for Undergraduate Students, but in 2006 the program was expanded to include graduate students financing their own educations. We cannot even begin to tell you how helpful this is for artists. Before 2006, most graduate students took out private loans to help cover living expenses. Now they have the option of PLUS Loans. These loans were also tied to the financial markets as part of the Bipartisan Student Loan Certainty Act of 2013, and the rates are recalculated each year. For 2016-2017 they have an interest rate of 6.31% and an origination fee of 4.276%. An **origination** fee, remember, is an activation fee charged at the beginning of a transaction with a bank. An origination fee of 4% is significant: by comparison Stafford Loans have an origination fee of around 1%. The interest rate for PLUS Loans is unsubsidized, so interest has been accruing on these loans while you've been in school, just like the interest on your unsubsidized Stafford Loans did. Prepare for a certain amount of sticker shock here as well. But the good news is that, for graduate students, PLUS Loans can be consolidated with all other government loans, giving you much more flexible repayment options than private loans. They can be included in the income-based repayment plans we will discuss later in this book, which

14

may make your budget and life as an artist easier in your first few years out of school. However, you should know that PLUS Loans taken out by parents for undergraduate expenses *cannot* be consolidated into these repayment plans. Technically, your parents owe these loans, not you.

Private Loans are student loans offered by private lending organizations to help defer the cost of education. PLUS Loans should eventually replace private loans completely (at least for graduate students) but if you have these loans, they will be the most difficult to repay. Most likely, you took them out to help pay for living expenses while you were in school. Every bank will have different fees and different repayment plans, often with higher interest rates and shorter repayment options. You may not be able to consolidate these loans with your current lender, and you cannot combine them with your federal loans.

Lenders and Servicers

When you graduate, or perhaps even before you graduate, you will start to receive envelopes in the mail from different servicers. Now, you may have assumed that all of your bills and notifications would come from the same company or organization. But the growing stack of envelopes on your desk might include letters from different companies: EdFinancial, Sallie Mae, Great Lakes Education, or Nelnet to name a few. Needless to say, this can get confusing. We're going to explain the difference between a lender and a servicer next, and then get you ready for consolidation.

A **lender** is the bank that initially loaned you money. They are the moneyman, Scrooge McDuck, the people who gave you cash so that you could go to school. A **servicer** is the organization that sends you statements and bills. They are the collection agency, the guy who knocks on your door, the people who collect your monthly payments. Depending on the size of the corporation, a bank might lend *and* service your loan. Private loan giants like Discover have their own servicing departments to handle the administrative work of billing and collection. The U.S. Department of Education, however, assigns Direct Loans to a separate loan servicer, outsourcing the work to a private company. If you watched *The Sopranos* on HBO, think of it as the difference between Tony Soprano and Paulie. Tony (the lender) gives you the money, but he sends Paulie (the servicer) to collect.

The next complicated matter is that student loans are often sold from one bank to another. The government may also assign different servicers to different loans. You might have difficulty figuring out just exactly whom you owe money and where you should send your monthly payment. A lender *must send you documentation* notifying you if your loan is sold or if your servicer has changed, which is one more reason to open all those statements you get in the mail. You do not want to go into default simply because you couldn't figure out who you should pay.

Recent legislation has simplified the student loan process, basically forcing private lenders out of the federal loan market. In 1993 a law went into effect that created the Federal Direct Loan Program, in which the government not only guarantees student loans but is in fact the lender as well. A bill passed in 2010 made the FDLP the only government backed student loan program. That means that all new federal student loans (Stafford, Perkins, PLUS) are owned by the Department of Education as of July 2010, hopefully easing the confusion over lenders and servicers. The AFSG highly recommends consolidating all of your federal loans with the Direct Loan program, which will simplify the process further. Once you consolidate with the government, you should have one lender and one servicer. So let's get you ready for federal consolidation.

Now that you have a basic knowledge of what you're looking at when you view each loan statement, you should start to gather the information you need in order to consolidate. First, look through your statements again and figure out whether they are federal or private loans. If you're still confused as to which is which, your federal loans will have the label of Stafford, Perkins, or PLUS; any private loans will not. You'll need to identify five pieces of information for each loan, which should be clearly stated:

1. The Lender (who lent you the money)

2. The Servicer (who sends you statements)

3. The Loan Number (the number which identifies the specific loan)

4. The Interest Rate (the percentage fee charged annually for borrowing money)

5. The Current Loan Amount (how much you currently owe for each specific loan)

The government has a website that gathers information on all of your loans and lets you look at them in a simple, concise manner. You should still open all of your mail, but going to this website can be a helpful shortcut: **www.nslds.ed.gov**. Once you have the necessary information, you're ready for consolidation! Soon your loans will be under control and in repayment, and you'll breathe a lot easier.

Consolidation

What Happens Next?

You should now know what loans you have, as well as how interest has been accruing while you've been in school focusing on your art. What you need to figure out next is when repayment of your loans begins, and what your options are. You will have a grace period for most of your loans, but we strongly suggest starting the consolidation process as soon as possible for your federal loans. After consolidation you'll have the option of a number of different repayment plans, including several income-driven plans that base your payment not on how much money you owe, but rather on how much money you make. Regardless of the plan you choose, the last thing you want to do is ignore the letters on your desk, because they won't go away by themselves. You need to understand your options and get to work. Everything may seem a little complicated, but we're here to help. What happens next? Consolidation.

The Grace Period

A **grace period** refers to an optional period of time at the beginning of repayment during which the lender does not require payment from the borrower (that would be you). We suggest you think of it not as a grace period, but as a **prepare period**. Don't use this time to relax, use it instead to prepare yourself for consolidation and repayment. All Stafford Loans have a grace period of six months. PLUS Loans for graduate students (disbursed on or after July 1, 2008) have a "post-enrollment deferment period" of six months, which is basically the same thing as a grace period. Parents who have taken out PLUS Loans can request a similar six-month deferment. What exactly does that mean? You don't *have* to make payments on any of these loans until six months after graduation, though interest will continue to accrue on unsubsidized loans (and for subsidized loans taken out between July 1, 2012 and July 1, 2014). So if you're graduating in May, you don't need to start paying back these federal loans until November. Perkins Loans have a longer grace period: nine months. Private loans are different, and we'll talk about those separately. But for your federal loans, you can use the grace period to choose a repayment plan and familiarize yourself with your options. The process of consolidation will take 30-60 days according to the government, but may take up to three months. It will undoubtedly take longer than you expect, so don't put it off. We suggest starting consolidation no later than September, though the earlier the better. As with all bureaucratic processes, after you fill out the forms it will take a while for the government to process them. Once you consolidate, your loans will go into repayment, and you will begin to get monthly bills. The consolidation process itself is fairly simple and can be done online, which is what we recommend.

We'll say this several more times: *it is always better to know the details of your loans than to pretend they don't exist.* We can almost promise that you will have anxiety about that pile of envelopes, but know that this is completely normal. You might feel tightness in your chest or even sweat a little bit. Avoidance will seem like a very attractive option, but believe us, it is not a good idea. Even though this handbook has been meticulously researched, you need to pay attention to the details of your individual loans. For instance, prior to

July 1, 2008, graduate PLUS Loans did not have a grace period. For a few years these loans went into repayment almost immediately, 45 days after graduation. Many students during the transition had different PLUS Loans with and without grace periods, which they didn't realize. Suddenly they began receiving bills and phone calls asking for large amounts of money, during what they thought was their grace period. Now this should not happen to you, if your loans began after July 1, 2008. But it shows how important paying attention to the details will be as you navigate your financial life. The government has a telephone hotline you can call and ask any question, no matter how simple. For information on federal loans, you can call 1-800-848-0979 or visit **www.direct.ed.gov**.

What Exactly Is Consolidation?

Consolidation basically means combining smaller loans into one larger loan. Every semester you have taken out numerous loans: subsidized and unsubsidized Stafford Loans, and perhaps PLUS Loans or private loans. The average undergraduate student in the arts will have signed for one of each of these loans every year, meaning that when you graduate you will probably have four subsidized Stafford Loans and four unsubsidized Stafford Loans. Graduate students will most likely have three unsubsidized Staffords and three PLUS Loans. If you consolidate your federal loans, you basically combine these six to eight loans into one single loan, and then make one simple payment each month (Remember, private loans and Parent PLUS Loans cannot be consolidated with your government loans). What complicates consolidation is that the loans you have taken out have slightly different interest rates. In past years, interest rates for subsidized Stafford Loans have varied considerably: 3.4%, 3.86%, 4.66%, 4.29%, and 3.76%. Unsubsidized Stafford Loans were once consistent at a 6.8% interest rate, but now change each year and are currently 3.76% for undergraduates and 5.31% for graduate students. PLUS Loans were similarly a consistent 7.9% but are now 6.31%. When you combine the loans through consolidation, a new interest rate will be set that should fall somewhere in between all those individual rates. If you're very savvy, you may not want to consolidate in order to keep lower interest rates on certain loans. Or you can choose to consolidate some (but not all) of your loans, leaving out a specific loan that has an especially low rate. Finally, know that once you consolidate your loans you cannot reverse the process.

Now if you took out loans prior to 2010, consolidation may give you access to better repayment plans. Almost all government student loans dispersed after 2010 are part of the Federal Direct Loan Program (FDLP) and are eligible for all income-driven repayment plans, whether or not they are consolidated. Prior to 2010, government loans were also issued by another program called the Federal Family Education Loan (FFEL) Program. The only income-driven repayment plan open to borrowers of FFEL loans is Income Based Repayment (IBR). However, if you consolidate your FFEL loans into a Direct Consolidated Loan, you can use any of the income-driven plans. Similarly, Perkins Loans are not eligible for any income-driven plan unless they are consolidated.

If you decide that consolidation is right for you, start the process and before your grace period ends.

The consolidation process can be done online at: **www.studentloans.gov**, or you can also download a hard copy from the website, fill it out by hand, and mail it into their offices. We would recommend applying online, as it is relatively simple. You can save your application while you are filling it out online, so if you need to look up some information (or take a breather for a few minutes and scroll through your newsfeed on Facebook), you can do so and return to the application at any time. Before you consolidate, you will need to find your Federal Student Aid ID, which you use each year to apply for financial aid. The FSA ID replaced the FSA PIN in 2015, meaning that borrowers now pick a username and password instead of having to remember an arbitrary four-digit code. If you forget your password, go to **https://fsaid.ed.gov**.

After gathering all of the necessary information about your loans (which again, can easily be found online at **www.nslds.ed.gov**) you should be ready to start the consolidation process. If so, move on to the next section, which discusses the various repayment options. However, know that after the grace period there are two other options if you are simply unable to make your loan payments. We don't recommend them unless absolutely necessary, but they can be important tools if you need them. They can keep you from defaulting on your loans, which is something you definitely want to avoid. They are called deferment and forbearance.

Deferment

A **deferment** is a period in which repayment is postponed temporarily for specific situations, such as unemployment or economic hardship, or enrollment in school. While you have been in school, some of your loans have been in deferment already. Similar to the grace period, the *interest accruing on (most) subsidized loans will be paid by the government* during deferment, but the *interest on your unsubsidized loans will not*, and will eventually be capitalized, or added to your loan. Again, **capitalization** means that unpaid interest is folded into the base amount of your loan, causing the loan to increase in size. The two deferments that will be most helpful for you are the Unemployment Deferment and Economic Hardship Deferment.

Unemployment Deferment.   Like it or not, you may often be unemployed if you pursue a career in the arts. Artists qualify for this deferment quite easily. You must meet the following conditions: 1) You must be looking for full-time employment. 2) You must be registered with an employment agency that is actively trying to find you work. If you have representation as an artist, like an agent or manager, this certainly counts. 3) If you are receiving unemployment benefits, this will automatically qualify you. Simply supply documentation from the government that you are receiving unemployment benefits. Unemployment deferments are granted in six-month increments.

Economic Hardship Deferment.   You will automatically qualify if you receive federal or state public assistance benefits, or if you currently serve as a Peace Corps volunteer. You may also qualify if you work full time and your total monthly gross income is less than or equal to the monthly minimum wage rate, or 150% of the Poverty Guideline amount for your family size and state. The federal minimum wage is $7.25 in an hour in 2017, or $1,256.67 a month. The Poverty Guideline for the Contiguous 48 States and DC in 2017 is $12,060 a year for a family of one. 150% of that amount would be $18,090 per year (again for a family of one). Economic hardship deferments are granted in twelve-month increments.

Deferment is an option, but know that it is not free. We do not recommend deferring your loans if you are able to make payments on an income-driven repayment plan. You will continue to accrue interest on your unsubsidized loans while in deferment. If you have large loans, that accrued interest will be a significant amount of money added to your principal. Always defer before defaulting (simply not making payments), and never ignore your loans. The last avoidance option is forbearance.

Forbearance

Forbearance is a temporary postponement or reduction of payments for a period of time because you are experiencing financial difficulty. You don't want to go into forbearance unless you have already exhausted your deferments. Unlike deferment, *the government will not pay any of the interest accruing on your loans* during forbearance. You can forbear your loans in intervals of twelve months at a time. You may be required to pay a portion of your loan payment, or you may not have to pay anything. However, your loan will continue to increase in size, as the interest will capitalize. Again, we do not recommend forbearance, except in extreme circumstances. Private lenders may also have forbearance plans, but these should be a last resort.

Repayment

Choosing the Right Plan for You

Hopefully, the details of your student loans are starting to come into clearer focus. You've opened the letters on your desk, understand what they mean, and are no longer afraid of their contents. Well, maybe that's a little too much to ask, since almost all of us still get that nervous feeling in our chests from time to time. But like LeVar Burton used to say on Reading Rainbow, knowledge is power. At the end of the consolidation process online, you will need to choose a repayment plan. You should carefully take a look at all of them, and select the plan best for your circumstances. If you don't have very much loan debt, and you can afford the monthly payments, you should definitely choose Standard or Extended Repayment. *However, for those with a significant student loan burden, income-driven repayment plans may provide better options.* Remember, you just went to school to be an artist, and you need to be able to afford to be an artist. If you have incredibly high monthly payments, you will be forced to turn down low-paying jobs that might jump-start your career. You can always switch repayment plans, but at the beginning of your career, choose a plan that gives you financial flexibility.

As an example we'll use a consolidated loan of $100,000 with an interest rate of 5% to give you an idea of what payments might be like. Your own federal loans will have different interest rates and will be for larger or smaller amounts. We recommend using the repayment calculator on the government website to find out the specifics for your circumstances and determine your monthly payment under each plan. We used that calculator to give you the estimates listed. Find it at **www.studentaid.ed.gov**.

The Basic Repayment Plans

Standard Repayment. With the standard plan, you'll pay a fixed amount each month until your loans are paid in full. You'll have 10 years to repay your loans, which is probably the shortest term available. If you have taken out only a small amount in loans, this is probably your best option. But if you have a large debt load like many artists finishing school, this plan will have an astronomical monthly payment because the term is short. With a loan of $100,000 at 5%, you will have a monthly payment of $1,061.

Extended Repayment. Under the extended plan, you'll pay your loan over a period not to exceed 25 years. You must have more than $30,000 in loans to qualify, which is quite possible. Your monthly payments will be less than the standard plan because the term of the loan is longer (25 years as opposed to 10 years). However, you'll pay more over the life of the loan because more interest will accrue. If you have taken out a moderate amount in loans, this option may be right for you. If the monthly payment is still too high, consider the following options. Continuing with our example loan of $100,000 at 5% interest, your monthly payment will be $585.

Graduated Repayment. With this plan, your payments start out low and increase every two years. The length of the repayment period can be either of the previous plans, standard (10 years) or extended (25 years). This plan is generally for people who expect their income to increase steadily over time, which is not necessarily true for artists.

Using our example of a $100,000 loan at 5%, your loan payment on Standard Graduated Repayment would begin at $600 a month and grow to $1,800 a month. With Extended Graduated Repayment, payments would start at $417 and grow to $951 a month. We don't think this is a plan you'll want to utilize, as there are better options.

The Income-Driven Repayment Plans

The income-driven repayment plans all base your monthly payment not on how much you owe, but rather on how much money you make. Each year, your payment is recalculated using your income from the previous year (as reported by your taxes). If you have significant debt, *the AFSG recommends starting your artistic career on an income-driven plan.* These plans will almost certainly give you the lowest monthly payment, providing flexibility in your budget as you get on your feet both financially and artistically. You shouldn't have to turn down prestigious jobs or fellowships that don't pay well, simply because you can't afford your high student loan payments. You went to school to be an artist, so be an artist. Take the jobs that will help you build your resume and make connections. If you allow yourself to take these opportunities, they will hopefully lead to higher-paying artistic work and career advancement.

Despite the advantages, you should know that your smaller payments come at a cost. If you choose an income-driven plan, you may end up in **negative amortization**. What does that mean? Amortization is a fancy word for loan repayment, and derives from the Latin "mort" which means death. Imagine your loan as a monster. With each payment in amortization, you injure the loan monster with your sword, until eventually it dies. Negative amortization would then mean the opposite: instead of injuring the monster, you just make it angry, and stronger. The loan actually gets larger instead of smaller. Why? With such a small monthly payment, you may not be paying enough to even cover the interest accruing. Each year that unpaid interest may make your loan grow in size even though you are making steady monthly payments. If that scares you a little: good (it should scare you). As your income increases however, the size of your payment will also increase, and this trend may reverse itself. Eventually, if you start making serious money, we recommend that you transition into a more stable repayment option like Standard Repayment.

But what if things don't turn out the way you hope and your income never increases substantially? Don't panic. If you make steady payments on an income-driven plan over the course of the loan term (usually 20 or 25 years), any balance remaining on your loan will eventually be forgiven. Yes, you read that correctly: *forgiven*. The amount forgiven will be considered taxable income (so it's still complicated), but more on that later. If you choose an income-driven plan, just know that the benefits all come with certain disadvantages as well. Make your decision carefully.

Remember, all new government student loans as of 2010 are part of the Direct Loan program. Borrowers who took out loans prior to 2010 may have done so through the Federal Family Education Loan (FFEL) Program. The only income-driven plan that allows an FFEL loan is Income-Based Repayment (IBR). However, if you combine your individual FFEL loans into a consolidated Direct Loan, you will then have access to the other plans.

Now that we've gone over the basics of income-driven repayment, lets look at the individual plans.

Revised Pay As You Earn. REPAYE is the newest plan, and it's available to all borrowers with Direct Loans with no income requirements. Basically, anyone can get onto this plan. Your monthly payment is calculated as 10% of your discretionary income. For our example lets say that you have an income of $40,000 (adjusted after tax deductions to $36,000) with a $100,000 consolidated loan at 5% interest. Your monthly payment on REPAYE would be $149. Now that sounds better, right? Keep in mind, though, that your payments may not cover the interest accruing and your loan may grow in size. *But a remarkable benefit of REPAYE addresses that exact problem:* if your payment doesn't cover the interest accruing, the government pays the difference on subsidized loans for the first three years, after which it will pay half. For unsubsidized loans, the government will always pay half of the accrued interest not covered by your monthly payments. The interest benefit of REPAYE considerably slows the problem of negative amortization and limits the growth of your loan. The term of the loan is 20 years for undergraduate borrowers, but 25 years for any loans received for graduate or professional study. If you don't pay off the loan within that time, the remaining balance is forgiven (but considered taxable income).

Pay As You Earn. If you want to use the PAYE plan, your income must be low compared to your eligible federal student loan debt and you must have Direct Loans. You must also be a new borrower as of October 1, 2007 and received the disbursement of a Direct Loan on or after October 1, 2011. Your monthly payment is calculated as 10% of your discretionary income, the same as it is on the REPAYE plan. However, on PAYE your payments will never be more than it would be on a 10-year Standard Repayment Plan. If you start making a significantly larger amount of money, your payment is effectively capped at that fixed amount. With an income of $40,000 (adjusted to $36,000 after deductions) and a $100,000 consolidated loan at 5% interest, your monthly payment on PAYE is $149. Remember, your loan may grow in size due to negative amortization. If your monthly payment doesn't cover the interest accruing on subsidized loans, the government pays the difference for the first three years. After those three years, the interest will again become your responsibility. The loan term is 20 years for undergraduate and graduate borrowers, after which the remaining balance is forgiven (but considered taxable income).

Income-Based Repayment. Similar to PAYE, there is an income requirement for IBR. Your income must be low compared to your eligible federal student loan debt. You can use this plan with loans from either Direct Loans or FFEL. The plan also effectively divides borrowers into two groups, those who took out loans on or after July 1, 2014 (considered new borrowers) and those who took out loans prior to July 1, 2014. For new borrowers, your payment is calculated as 10% of your discretionary income. For everyone else, payment is 15% of discretionary income. Like PAYE, IBR caps your monthly payment so that it is never more than what you would pay on a 10-year Standard Repayment Plan. Continuing our example of a $100,000 loan at 5% and an income of $40,000 (adjusted after tax deductions to $36,000), your monthly payment on IBR is $149 for new borrowers, $224 for everyone else. If your monthly payment doesn't cover the full amount of interest accruing on your subsidized loans, the government will pay the difference for the first three years. After those three years, the interest is your responsibility. The loan term is 20 years for new borrowers and 25 years for borrowers with loans prior to 2014. Again, the remaining balance is forgiven (but considered taxable income).

Income-Contingent Repayment. ICR is the original income-driven plan, and it's available to all borrowers with Direct Loans with no additional requirements. Your monthly payment is calculated as 20% of your income. With an income of $40,000 (adjusted after tax deductions to $36,000), using our example of a $100,000 consolidated loan at 5%, your monthly payment on the ICR will be $399. Again, your loan may grow in size if your payments don't cover the interest. And importantly, the ICR does not offer any interest benefit. If your monthly payment doesn't cover the interest accruing on your loan, you are responsible for paying that interest from the very beginning of repayment. If you are in negative amortization, your loan will grow quickly on this plan. The loan term is 25 years, after which the balance is forgiven (but considered taxable income).

We'll discuss the differences between REPAYE, PAYE, IBR, and ICR in more detail in the next chapter, and give you the algorithms that calculate your monthly payments. We'll show you the math, and we'll continue the discussion about the financial decisions you will be making by entering into any of these four plans. Again, if you can afford the payments on Standard Repayment, you should strongly consider using that option. Remember, on an income-driven plan, negative amortization may cause your loan to grow in size even though you're making steady payments. You need to look carefully at the details of these plans and choose the one that best fits your circumstances. For those considering an income-driven plan, *we usually recommend REPAYE because of its lower payments and interest benefits, and*

PAYE or IBR(NB) for graduate students because of their shorter loan term of 20 years and quicker path to forgiveness.

Monthly Payments

After you have consolidated your loans and entered repayment, you will need to make payments every month. We highly recommend doing this online, thereby eliminating the envelopes that we've been talking about, and the pile on your desk. You will receive a simple email reminder every month, log onto the government website, and pay your bill. Or you can set up automatic payment, which will lower your interest rate by 0.25%. As an artist you will most likely travel often, leaving town for work in different cities. You do not want to return to your apartment after months out of town and then realize you are delinquent because you forgot to pay your loans. If you have trouble paying your loans during difficult times, know that there are two other options that we previously discussed: deferment and forbearance. We don't recommend them unless absolutely necessary, but they can be important tools if you need them. *The worst possible thing to do is ignore your loans and then default.* Call the government hotline and talk to someone about your options. Always defer before you forbear, and forbear before you default.

Private Loans

Advice about private loans is complicated. Before PLUS Loans, many undergraduate and graduate students in the arts took out private loans through programs like CitiAssist at Citibank, meant to help cover living expenses. For many undergraduates, private loans continue to be the only option available to fully afford the cost of college if parents do not want to commit to PLUS Loans. We can't write too much about the specifics of private loans, because depending on the lender you chose, the terms and rates will vary significantly. However, in the current financial landscape of 2017, many private lenders may offer loans at better rates than the government. Do your research. If you are only taking out a moderate amount of loans, it may be possible to save money by borrowing from private lenders.

However, unlike government loans, it is quite possible that those private loans will have variable interest rates, which will cause your payments to fluctuate with the market. Look into the details of these loans very carefully, and pay attention to the repayment plans offered. *Know that private loans cannot be consolidated into government repayment options.* You will not find income-based repayment plans like REPAYE or the IBR at private lenders. You might not be able to consolidate these loans even with your lender. After the financial crisis of 2008, many private lenders refused to offer consolidation or extended repayment plans. Many artists have private loans locked into 10-year or 15-year repayment plans, and monthly payments that comprise a significant portion of their budgets. The untenable situation of private loans heavily influenced the formation of the Artists Financial Support Group.

Private lenders, unlike the government, will be less flexible and more aggressive. *You do not want to default on your private loans.* Artists who have defaulted on their private loans have been pursued by collection agencies, called multiple times daily by their lenders, and had their wages garnished. If you have private loans, *always pay these first.* Go into deferment or forbearance with the government, but do not default on private loans.

The Math

How Do the Income-Driven Plans Work?

What you will find in this chapter is an in-depth look at the income-driven repayment plans offered by the government that base your monthly payment on your yearly income. The language used by the government to describe these programs is particularly dense, but we will attempt to explain everything as simply as possible. *Know that the AFSG usually recommends REPAYE because of its lower payments and interest benefits. However, for borrowers with debt from graduate school, PAYE and IBR for New Borrowers offer a shorter loan term of 20 years and a quicker path to forgiveness.* If you need the lowest monthly payment possible, these plans will be the best for you. Always choose these plans over deferment or forbearance. However, do not choose these plans lightly. Staying on income-based repayment indefinitely can have serious consequences, including the growth of your loan due to negative amortization. If possible, try to at least cover the interest each year on your loans, even if it means paying more than your required monthly payment.

Before we get started, something to remember: *You must resubmit documentation of your income each year in order to stay on these plans.* If you don't recertify your income, your monthly payment will increase substantially. Do not procrastinate! When you get an email asking for the information, submit a copy of your tax return promptly online.

If the financial jargon and the math in this chapter start to make your head spin, hang in there. As an organization, the Artists Financial Support Group (AFSG) strongly believes in **financial self-advocacy**, the assertion of self-determination and personal responsibility in your financial life. The income-driven plans all offer slightly different benefits and risks. The more you know about your loans, the more control and confidence you will have. We strongly encourage you to read the following section and learn the details of these different plans. While we acknowledge that the information is complicated, we will try to explain everything as simply as we can in the following pages.

REPAYE, PAYE, IBR and ICR are repayment options that base your monthly payment on your annual income. They were designed to help people going into public service, as well as those with a high debt-to-income ratio (I'm looking at you, recently graduated artist). Your repayment amount is adjusted annually: It is higher when your income for the year is higher, and lower when your income for the year is lower. The adjustments are made each year when you submit documentation of your taxes. If you make regular payments over the loan term (usually 20 or 25 years) but do not pay off the entirety of the loan, *the balance is then forgiven* (though considered taxable income). The AFSG usually recommends REPAYE, but all four plans can be invaluable in lowering your monthly payment and giving you financial flexibility. Let's take a look at the differences between the REPAYE, PAYE, IBR and ICR plans, which are subtle but quite important.

Getting on the Plans

Revised Pay As You Earn (REPAYE). Anyone with Direct Loans can sign up for REPAYE. There are no additional income restrictions or requirements.

Pay As You Earn (PAYE). If you want to choose PAYE you must be a *new borrower* as of Oct. 1, 2007, and you must have received the disbursement of a Direct Loan on or after Oct. 1, 2011. Basically, this means that you have to have graduated in 2012 or after in order to sign up for Pay As You Earn. PAYE has an income requirement as well: you must experience **partial financial hardship**. A partial financial hardship is defined as "a circumstance in which the annual amount due on all your eligible loans at the time you enter repayment, as calculated under a 10-year Standard Repayment Plan, exceeds 15 percent of the difference between your AGI and 150% of the poverty line income for your family size." What the hell does that mean? It means that if your payments on a 10-year Standard Repayment plan are more than what your payments would be calculated on the PAYE plan, you can be on PAYE. If you took out a substantial amount of loans in order to get an undergraduate or graduate degree in the arts, you will most likely qualify for PAYE.

Income-Based Repayment (IBR). Borrowers with both Direct Loans *and* FFEL Loans can qualify for IBR, making it unique among the income-driven plans. Like PAYE, you need to experience partial financial hardship. What does that mean? Basically, if you would pay less on IBR than you would on Standard Repayment, you qualify.

Income-Contingency Repayment (ICR). Anyone with Direct Loans can sign up for ICR. There are no additional income restrictions or requirements.

How Are Payments Calculated?

All four plans base your monthly payments on a percentage of your discretionary income. But they calculate that discretionary income in slightly different ways. Before we get started, we should define a few terms.

Adjusted gross income is the money you make in a year, minus tax deductions. The **poverty level** is the minimum level of income necessary for an adequate standard of living, as determined each year by the government. **Discretionary income** is the amount of money you have left to spend after paying for essentials like food, clothing, and shelter. With those definitions in order, we can continue our discussion.

Payment on REPAYE and PAYE is 10% of your monthly discretionary income, and that income is calculated as your federal Adjusted Gross Income minus 150% of the poverty level. Payment on IBR is 15% of your monthly discretionary income, with that income calculated using the same formula as PAYE. Payment on ICR is 20% of your monthly discretionary income, but that income is calculated differently, as your AGI minus the poverty level.

Let's take an example and compare the plans. In this example, we'll say that you made $40,000 last year. After deductions, you get your AGI down to $36,000. We'll use the U.S. Poverty Guidelines for the Contiguous 48 States and DC in 2017 for our calculations: $12,060 for a family of one. Below you will see how each plan determines your yearly discretionary income. You should notice right away that the calculation of your discretionary income, based on the exact same yearly earnings, is much less under the REPAYE, PAYE, and IBR plans than it is under ICR.

DISCRETIONARY INCOME
(AGI of $36,000 in using 2017 guidelines)

REPAYE = AGI -1.5 x Poverty Level
= $36,000 - (1.5 x $12,060)
= $17,910

PAYE = AGI -1.5 x Poverty Level
= $36,000 - (1.5 x $12,060)
= $17,910

IBR = AGI -1.5 x Poverty Level
= $36,000 - (1.5 x $12,060)
= $17,910

ICR = AGI - Poverty Level
= $36,000 - $12,060
= $23,940

Next, let's take into account the percentage of your discretionary income you are expected to pay. It gets a little more complicated here, as IBR is essentially two separate plans: one for new borrowers who took out loans on or after July 1, 2014 and another for everyone who took out loans prior to that date (for clarity, we'll refer to "IBR for New Borrowers" as IBR(NB) from here on out). The percentage of your discretionary income you are expected to pay is 10% for REPAYE, PAYE and IBR(NB), 15% for IBR, and 20% for ICR. Below you will see how your monthly payments are calculated on each of the plans.

MONTHLY PAYMENT
(Example loan of $100,000 at 5%, AGI of $36,000)

REPAYE = (10% of Discretionary Income)/12
= (.1 x $17,910)/12
= $149.25

PAYE = (10% of Discretionary Income)/12
= (.1 x $17,910)/12
= $149.25

IBR(NB) = (10% of Discretionary Income)/12
= (.1 x $17,910)/12
= $149.25

IBR = (15% of Discretionary Income)/12
= (.15 x $17,910)/12
= $223.88

ICR = (20% of Discretionary Income)/12
= (.2 x $23,940)/12
= $399.00

REPAYE, PAYE, and IBR(NB) offer the lowest monthly payment, followed by IBR, and then ICR. Now these monthly payments hold true *regardless of how much money you owe.* How can that be possible? Well, it's time to return to that fun subject, negative amortization!

Negative Amortization

Again, we cannot stress enough that on these plans your payments may not even cover the interest on your loans. With all of these plans, this may eventually lead to **negative**

amortization and the growth of your loans even while in repayment (though it works differently on each plan). Remember, amortization is an SAT vocab word that means loan repayment, and derives from the Latin "mort" which means death. Every time you make a payment in amortization, you stab a sword into the monster that is your loan, until eventually you kill it. With negative amortization, you are still making payments, but when you stab your sword into the monster you just make it angry – and larger. The unpaid interest will cause your loan to grow in size even though you are making steady monthly payments. The smaller your monthly payment, the less interest you are paying, and the larger your loan will grow. The very benefit of lower payment, then, directly causes the problems of negative amortization and capitalization.

Most of these plans attempt to address the problem of negative amortization through interest subsidies. REPAYE overwhelmingly offers the best option to help borrowers control the problem of increasing loan size due to low monthly payments and unpaid interest. *This incredible interest benefit is the reason why we usually recommend REPAYE for borrowers who need an income-driven plan.* With REPAYE, the government pays any unpaid interest on your subsidized loans (and half of the unpaid interest for your unsubsidized loans) for the first three years of repayment. After three years, the government will pay half the unpaid interest on all of your loans for the remainder of your loan term. We'll explain just how remarkable that is in a moment.

With PAYE, IBR(NB), and IBR the government pays any unpaid interest on subsidized loans (but not unsubsidized loans) for the first three years of repayment. After those initial three years, all unpaid interest is your responsibility.

With ICR there is no interest benefit: if your monthly payment doesn't cover the full amount of the interest accruing on your loans, you're responsible for paying it.

INTEREST BENEFITS

REPAYE
The government pays the full amount of unpaid interest on your subsidized loans (and half the unpaid interest on your unsubsidized loans) for three years. After three years, they pay half the unpaid interest on all your loans.

PAYE, IBR(NB), IBR
The government pays the full amount of your unpaid interest on your subsidized loans for three years.

ICR
The government provides no interest benefit.

What exactly does this all mean? Let's return to our example of a federal loan of $100,000 and an interest rate of 5%. We'll first look at what happens in the very first year of repayment, during which PAYE, IBR(NB), and IBR all provide interest subsidies, and for this example we will say that all of your loans are subsidized. You almost certainly will have unsubsidized loans as well, but for this example let's try to keep things simple. With an income of $40,000 (adjusting your AGI to $36,000 after deductions), you will pay $149.25 a month on REPAYE, PAYE, and IBR(NB). You will pay $223.88 on IBR, and $399 on ICR. The loans accrue $5,000 of interest in that first year. How does this cause negative amortization?

LOAN GROWTH IN FIRST YEAR
(Example Loan of $100,000 at 5%, AGI of $36,000)

REPAYE = $149.25 monthly payment
  Interest paid = 12 x $149.25   = $1,791
  Unpaid interest = $5,000 - $1,791 = $3,209
  Government pays 100% interest = $3,209
  New loan balance = $100,000

PAYE = $149.25 monthly payment
  Interest paid = 12 x $149.25   = $1,791
  Unpaid interest = $5,000 - $1,791 = $3,209
  Government pays 100% interest = $3,209
  New loan balance = $100,000

IBR(NB)= $149.25 monthly payment
  Interest paid = 12 x $149.25   = $1,791
  Unpaid interest = $5,000 - $1,791 = $3,209
  Government pays 100% interest = $3,209
  New loan balance = $100,000

IBR = $223.88 monthly payment
  Interest paid = 12 x $223.88 = $2,686.56
  Unpaid interest = $5,000 - $2,686.56 = $2,313.44
  Government pays 100% interest = $2,313.44
  New loan balance = $100,000

ICR = $399 monthly payment
  Interest paid = 12 x $399 = $4,788
  Unpaid interest = $5,000 - $4,788 = $212
  New loan balance = $100,212

Your $100,000 loan has grown in size only on ICR, and just slightly. The larger payment of ICR offsets the lack of subsidy, increasing your loan by an amount of $212. With REPAYE, PAYE, IBR(NB) and IBR, your loan does not grow in the first year, though it does hold steady at $100,000 despite your monthly payments. Remember, though, that the interest subsidy for PAYE, IBR(NB) and IBR only helps with the first three years of repayment. And after three years, REPAYE only covers half of the interest. The effects of negative amortization only become clear as we get further into the life of the loan, after year three.

So let's look again at our example of an initial $100,000 subsidized loan at 5% interest in the fourth year of repayment, after the 100% unpaid interest subsidy for PAYE, IBR(NB) and IBR ends. The subsidy on REPAYE no longer covers all of the unpaid interest, but will continue to pay 50% of any unpaid interest not covered by your monthly payment. For consistency, we will keep your income the same at $40,000 (reduced to an AGI of $36,000 after tax deductions). Let's take a look at how the different plans might work in the fourth year of the loan.

If you look closely at the numbers below, you will see that your loan grows the slowest on ICR because of its larger payment. REPAYE has next smallest balance, as PAYE, IBR(NB) and IBR now grow at a much faster rate because of the loss of the interest subsidy.

LOAN GROWTH IN YEAR FOUR
(Example Loan of $100,000 at 5%, AGI of $36,000)

REPAYE = $149.25 monthly payment
   Current balance = $100,000
   Unpaid interest = $5,000 - $1,791 = $3,209
   Government pays 50% interest = $3,209 x .5 = $1604.50
   Revised unpaid interest = $1,604.50
   New loan balance = $100,000 + ($1,604.50)

PAYE = $149.25 monthly payment
   Current balance = $100,000
   Interest paid = 12 x $149.25 = $1,791
   Unpaid interest = $5,000 - $1,791 = $3,209
   New loan balance = $100,000 + ($3,209)

IBR(NB) = $149.25 monthly payment
   Current balance = $100,000
   Interest paid = 12 x $149.25 = $1,791
   Unpaid interest = $5,000 - $1,791 = $3,209
   New loan balance = $100,000 + ($3,209)

IBR = $223.88 monthly payment
   Current balance = $100,000
   Interest paid = 12 x $223.88 = $2,686.56
   Unpaid interest = $5,000 - $2,686.56 = $2,313.44
   New loan balance = $100,000 + ($2,313.44)

ICR = $399 monthly payment
   Current balance = $100,668.33
   Interest paid = 12 x $399 = $4788
   Unpaid interest = $5033.42 - $4788 = $245.42
   New loan balance = $100,913.75

Let's pause here for a moment to talk more about unpaid interest and capitalization. With REPAYE, the unpaid interest is capitalized (added to the loan principal balance) only if you are removed from the plan for failing to recertify your income by the annual deadline or you voluntarily leave the plan. What exactly does that mean? Consider our example loan above. Despite making steady payments on REPAYE, we had unpaid interest in the amount of $3,209. The government paid half of the interest, but that still left us with $1,604.50 of unpaid interest. However, if you remain on REPAYE the interest doesn't capitalize. So technically, you would have a loan of $100,000 + ($1,604.50), with new interest only calculated on the $100,000 principal. The unpaid interest effectively floats next to your loan, separate from the principal. By allowing interest to accrue without capitalization, REPAYE keeps you from paying interest on interest.

PAYE, IBR(NB), and IBR work in a similar way. The unpaid interest does not capitalize until you no longer qualify to make payments based on your income or you leave the plan. Like REPAYE, the interest effectively floats next to the loan, separate from the principal. Unfortunately, ICR does not help at all with unpaid interest. If your monthly payment on ICR is less than the amount of interest that accrues on your loan, the unpaid interest capitalizes *every year*. Using our example, your loan principal on ICR has increased to $100,913.75. The interest does not float next to the principal, but is added to the principal. That said, ICR (and PAYE) limit the amount of interest that capitalizes to 10% of the original loan principal balance at the time you enter the plan. With REPAYE, IBR(NB) and IBR there are no limits to the amount capitalized.

LOAN GROWTH IN YEAR TEN
(Example Loan of $100,000 at 5%, AGI of $36,000)

REPAYE = $149.25 monthly payment
  Current balance = $100,000 + ($9,627)
  Interest paid = 12 x $149.25 = $1,791
  Unpaid interest = $5,000 - $1,791 = $3,209
  Government pays 50% interest = $3,209 x .5 = $1604.50
  Revised unpaid interest = $1,604.50
  New loan balance = $100,000 + ($11,231.50)

PAYE = $149.25 monthly payment
  Current balance = $100,000 + ($19,254)
  Interest paid = 12 x $149.25 = $1,791
  Unpaid interest = $5,000 - $1,791 = $3,209
  New loan balance = $100,000 + ($22,463)

IBR(NB)= $149.25 monthly payment
  Current balance = $100,000 + ($19,254)
  Interest paid = 12 x $149.25 = $1,791
  Unpaid interest = $5,000 - $1,791 = $3,209
  New loan balance = $100,000 + ($22,463)

IBR = $223.88 monthly payment
  Current balance = $100,000 + (13,880.64)
  Interest paid = 12 x $223.88 = $2,686.56
  Unpaid interest = $5,000 - $2,686.56 = $2,313.44
  New loan balance = $100,000 + ($16,194.08)

ICR = $399 monthly payment
  Current balance = $102,337.64
  Interest paid = 12 x $399 = $4788
  Unpaid interest = $5,116.88 - $4788 = $313.22
  New loan balance = $102,666.52

Take one last look at our example above that uses a $100,000 subsidized loan at 5% interest. We keep your income consistent at $40,000 (reduced to an AGI of $36,000 after tax deductions). After ten years of repayment, the differences in the plans become even clearer. REPAYE continues to pay half of all your unpaid interest, but on the rest of the income-driven plans you are responsible for paying all of the interest not covered by your monthly payment. Your loans on PAYE and IBR(NB) have grown to almost $22,000 more than the initial principal, even though you have made steady payments for ten years. With IBR it has grown by $16,000. Even with the interest subsidy, on REPAYE your loan has grown by $11,000. Your payment on ICR was the highest, and the loan grew by a much smaller amount, a little under $3,000.

Do you begin to see the serious consequences of negative amortization? The low payments offered by the income-driven plans provide financial freedom, but at a cost. With each plan, your loan grew in size. Now, most likely your income will increase over the years and cause the effects of your loan growth to slow or reverse. The poverty line also changes each year, which will alter the math above. But looking at this example, it should become clear which plans are best if you are unable to pay the interest accruing on your loans. ICR grows the slowest, because of its larger payment. REPAYE grows significantly, but at a much slower rate than PAYE, IBR(NB) and IBR. *The lower payments and interest benefits often make REPAYE the best option.*

You should now also understand why you might not want to stay on income-based repayment indefinitely. If your income does not increase to the point where your monthly payment at least pays the interest, your loan will continue to grow. When possible, try to pay at least the interest that accrues each year, in addition to your monthly payments. And if you can afford the payment amount, you should transition into Standard or Extended Repayment. If you are unable to do so, however, know that all is not lost.

Forgiveness (and Taxes)

If you make steady payments for the term of your loan while in income-driven repayment, your loans will be forgiven (after 20 or 25 years, depending on the program). Loan forgiveness, though remarkable, is not free. The forgiveness of your loans will be considered taxable income. What would that look like? Well, if you finish undergrad at 22 and make steady payments on REPAYE for 20 years, your loans will be forgiven when you are 42 years old. Maybe you are able to pay off half of our example student loan of $100,000 during the term of the loan, leaving you a balance of $50,000, which is forgiven. And let's say that at 42 years old you are married, and that you and your spouse make a combined $100,000 and file taxes jointly. The IRS will tax your income at $150,000 instead of $100,000. If we use the 2017 tax code (which will certainly change before your loans are forgiven), you would pay $28,977.50 in taxes that year instead of the $16,477.50 you would pay without forgiveness. Your forgiveness of $50,000 will cost you $12,500. You'll need to plan for this, but remember, the IRS has payment plans as well.

Let's try another example. What if your loans get away from you? You finish grad school at 27 and get on IBR, and your loans are forgiven after 25 years of steady repayment when you're 52. You were unable to pay the interest every year on our example loan, and it ballooned from $100,000 to

$164,000. And let's say when you're 52 you are single and still make $36,000. The IRS will tax your income at $200,000 instead of $36,000. Again using the 2017 tax code, you would owe $49,399.25 in taxes that year instead of the $4,933.75 you would owe without forgiveness. Your loan forgiveness of $164,000 would cost you $49,399.25.

The length of the loan term might give an advantage to PAYE and IBR(NB) for graduate students. The shorter repayment period means that you reach the possibility of forgiveness five years earlier than you would on REPAYE, IBR, or ICR. For undergraduate students several plans offer this advantage: REPAYE, PAYE, and IBR(NB) all provide forgiveness after 20 years for undergraduate debt. For undergraduates, REPAYE is clearly the best option.

FORGIVENESS

After steady repayment on an income-driven repayment plan, any remaining debt is forgiven at the end of your loan term. The different plans offer loan terms, meaning you may reach forgiveness faster on certain plans.

REPAYE

20 years for undergraduate loans, 25 for graduate loans.

PAYE

20 years for both undergraduate and graduate loans.

IBR(NB)

20 years for both undergraduate and graduate loans.

IBR

25 years for both undergraduate and graduate loans.

ICR

25 years for both undergraduate and graduate loans.

What If I Start Making More Money?

If your income increases throughout the years (and we certainly hope that it does), the income-driven repayment plans adjust in different ways. REPAYE and ICR do not cap the amount of your monthly payment. As your income increases, your monthly payment will stay fixed at 10% (REPAYE) or 20% (ICR) of your discretionary income. Your monthly payment will grow accordingly with no limit.

PAYE, IBR(NB), and IBR both effectively limit your monthly payment to the amount you would have paid under Standard Repayment on a 10-year repayment period based on what you owed when you entered income-driven repayment. What does that mean? If your calculated payment is more than you would be required to pay under 10-year Standard Repayment, your monthly payment will no longer be based on your income. Instead, it will change to that 10-year Standard Repayment Plan amount. You are not forced off the plan, and you don't lose any eligibility toward forgiveness. You simply pay that set amount for the remainder of your existing loan term. If a balance remains on your loan after 20 or 25 years, it is still forgiven. However, you might actually pay off your loan before forgiveness occurs. If your income decreases for any reason, you can recertify your income and once again have your payments based upon your income.

Recertification of Income

A requirement of every income-drive plan is that you must submit documentation of your income each year. The plans base your monthly payment on your adjusted gross income, as reported by your taxes. Your loan servicer should send you an email or letter to remind you, but it is your responsibility: *Don't forget to recertify your income!* If you forget, the consequences vary slightly depending on the plan. Regardless of the plan, you should expect a much higher payment immediately, and *any unpaid interest will capitalize*. REPAYE removes you from your plan and puts you into an "alternative repayment plan" very similar to Standard Repayment. Under PAYE, IBR(NB), IBR or the ICR you will remain on the plan, but your payment will no longer be based on your income. Instead, your monthly payment will be the amount you would pay under Standard Repayment with a 10-year repayment period, based on your loan balance when you entered the plan. If this happens to you and you can't afford the payment, apply for a brief deferment and then immediately recertify your income.

Marriage & Taxes

If you get married or have children, it will affect your income-driven payments. The equations used to calculate your monthly payment include the poverty level, which varies based on family size. The larger your family grows, the smaller your required payment will be.

If you're married, REPAYE uses the income of both you and your spouse to calculate your payment, regardless of whether you file a joint or separate federal income tax return. However, PAYE, IBR(NB), IBR, and ICR only use your income to calculate your payment if you file separate returns. You will lose certain tax advantages, but if only one spouse has loans, this may be a helpful option. If you file a joint return, the plans will use the income of both spouses.

Budget

Plan for Unpredictability

After reading the previous chapters, you should have an understanding of how your loans work and what you will need to do upon graduation. More than likely, you'll go through the process of consolidation and start repayment. If you have substantial debt, REPAYE or another income-driven plan will now make your monthly payments manageable, and you can focus on beginning your career as an artist. We should pause here briefly to acknowledge what exactly it is you have accomplished. *You are now in control of your loans: your loans no longer control you.* Even that pile of letters on your desk is gone, since you signed up to receive all further correspondence by email and to pay online. However, the complications of your financial life as an artist unfortunately do not end with consolidation. In this next chapter of advice we would like to share with you concerns planning a budget and adopting an attitude of financial self-advocacy. The AFSG isn't your dad, so you don't have to listen to us and you certainly don't have to clean your room or be home before midnight. But having been out of school for a few years, we might be able to help you avoid some of the mistakes we made, and start to prepare you for life after school. An essential part of life as an artist is learning to plan for unpredictability.

The average person who does *not* pursue a career in the arts will find a job with a fixed annual salary after graduating from school, and they will probably stay at that job as long as they like the work. Because of their fixed income, the process of planning a budget should be relatively easy. If they make $800 a week (after taxes), they will have a monthly budget of $3,200. After taking into account their basic monthly expenses it will be easy to determine their discretionary income. **Discretionary income** is the amount of money you have left to spend each month after paying for essentials like food, clothing, and shelter. With income and expenses relatively stable, the non-artist can plan accordingly: saving money for a car or a vacation, or beginning to set aside money for retirement. If you have a variable income, however (and I'm looking at you, recently graduated artist), it becomes much more difficult to plan a budget. Even if you're working consistently, you may be looking for a new job every three months. Each job that you land will have a different weekly salary, and in between those jobs you will need to use a combination of unemployment benefits and support jobs to balance your budget. As a theater actor, you may make $861 a week on a LORT B contract at a regional theater like the Long Wharf in March, only to make $400 a week on a LOA contract at a small New York theater like Rattlestick in April. As a non-union DP (directory of photography) on an independent film, you might make a rate of $300 a day for a twenty-day shoot, but the very next month you may get only $300 a week on unemployment. How can you plan your financial life with such inconsistency and unpredictability? We suggest something called the reverse budget.

The Reverse Budget

If most people start planning their budget by looking at their income, what we suggest you do is start your financial planning by looking at your spending. During your first few months out of school, keep track of everything you spend.

When you get your groceries at Trader Joe's, see a movie at the AMC Loews, or buy a cup of coffee at Starbucks, keep the receipt. If the sales representative doesn't immediately offer you a receipt, ask for one. When you get home each night, take the receipts out of your wallet and enter what you spent that day into a simple Excel spreadsheet. You can easily find Excel budget templates to use online. Separate your expenses into simple categories like the following: groceries, eating out, entertainment, alcohol, household, office, electricity, phone/internet, transportation, loans, rent, health insurance, and other.

Add any other categories you might consider important, and make notes in the document for each miscellaneous expense. After you've entered the information for the day, set aside any receipts that document tax-deductible purchases, and throw the rest of them away. What you will begin to see are your spending patterns. You will notice that certain categories are fixed expenses that stay the same each month, like your rent and your loan payments. You will also find that other categories vary significantly each month. You might realize that your habit of taking cabs at three in the morning makes a significant dent in your budget, or that the $4 latte from Starbucks you can't live without every morning translates to $120 a month (which might cost more than your phone bill). You may want to slowly adjust your spending, especially in the variable categories. If you decide to take the subway instead of getting a cab, you can then afford to buy that new pair of jeans that fits you so perfectly. Making coffee in a French press each morning might let you use that $120 to take your girlfriend out for dinner at a fancy restaurant. More importantly, you will begin to get an estimate of just exactly how much money you need to make each month to cover your expenses. You might notice that if you save a bit of your salary while working at the Long Wharf for $861 a week, you'll be able to take the job at The Rattlestick that only pays $400 a week. If you make $6000 with a $300 day rate over a twenty-day shoot as a DP, you should save that money in case you want to film your own project with little to no budget. You'll get a feel for how much freelance work you'll need in order to supplement your other work. Basically, you'll be doing the opposite of what most people do when they plan their finances. You will try to plan your income from your expenses, using a reverse budget.

You can do this only for the first few months, or you can continue to use a simple budget to help you plan your finances for the years to come. We also recommend web services like **mint.com**, which track your accounts and your spending for you. Whatever you decide, know that understanding where you spend your money will allow you to adjust your budget and use your income more precisely. Then you will be ready for financial self-advocacy.

Financial Self-Advocacy

As we continue to impart advice to you, financial self-advocacy will be the next idea to absorb. Not only should one practice self-advocacy in every aspect of life, one should certainly practice it in regard to all things financial. **Financial self-advocacy** is the assertion of self-determination and personal responsibility in your financial life. What does that mean? Well, is the interest rate on your credit card too high? Call the credit card company and ask for it to be lowered. Did the bank just charge you an unfair overdraft fee? Call the bank and ask for it to be given back to you. Need a few more days to make a loan payment? Call your lender and ask if you can have more time. Financial institutions may look big and fancy with all of their branches, websites, and commercials, but when it comes down to it (as with almost all financial transactions) *haggling is expected*. Whenever you feel like you or your money is being taken for a ride, pick up the phone and ask for what you want or need. If the person you talk to first can't give it to you, ask to speak with their boss; and if the boss can't help you either, ask for their boss. Don't worry about taking up their time; it's their job.

No matter how puny your finances may feel sometimes, financial institutions need your money to survive. And to be completely honest, if you've taken out a large amount of loans, the financial institutions will pay attention to you because they want their money back. You may not always get what you want, but you may get half. You may not always get a "yes, we can do that for you," but a "no" from a bank is about the least important thing in the world, and shouldn't affect your self-esteem. The feeling you will have when you hang up the phone after getting a fee refunded, negotiating a lower monthly payment, or securing a lower interest rate is worth all the no's you may get. The illusion of control is what financial institutions use to earn money, but in reality, you have more power than you think, and that power is called financial self-advocacy.

Financial Calendar

Do you have a calendar? Is it on your phone, your computer, or is it the old-fashioned paper variety? How many times have you written down financial deadlines in your calendar? Now is the time is the time to start.

When is your loan payment due? Let's say it is the 9th of every month. Write that down in your calendar, every month, so it doesn't sneak up on you. When is your credit card bill due? The 6th? Write it down, every month. When do you need to certify your unemployment benefits every week, so that there's no interruption in your payments? Every Sunday, you say? Write it down, every week. When during your billing cycle did the telephone operator from the credit card company suggest you call to ask for a lower interest rate? The 15th of every month? Brilliant, now you know! Write it down, and do it every month.

Does your e-calendar have an alarm function? Use it. Know when your financial deadlines are happening every week of every month of every year. If you don't know, call and ask! When you pay off your loans, don't need unemployment, and have a single digit interest rate on your credit card (with no balance, of course), you can marvel at how clear your calendar is, and fill it with the things that truly matter.

The Credit Card Freeze

Credit cards - we love them and we hate them. Impossible to build credit without them (but easy to fall into the traps for which they are designed), credit cards can separate you from money you don't even have yet. Responsible credit card use is imperative. Everything you buy (even if it's on sale) ends up costing significantly more if you carry a balance and pay high interest rates. Get out of credit card debt, and then try to pay off your balance each month. Using your card, however, does help you build a good credit score. Is there an expense you pay automatically every month? A phone bill, rent on a storage locker, or your Netflix account? Set up automatic payments with your credit card, but only if you have the real money to back it up. That way you will continue to build credit, but you'll do it using money that you actually have.

What's that you say? Your credit card seems to jump out of your wallet and take on a life of its own? Did you buy a couch, pick up a few rounds of drinks at the bar, or pay more than full price for a ticket to a sold-out concert? STOP. Do you have the actual money to pay for it? If not, consider putting that credit card in some Tupperware, filling it with water, and throwing it in the freezer. Your automatic costs will continue to accrue and you'll be able to pay them off with actual money each month, but you won't buy things you can't afford. If the moment comes when you absolutely need to use that card, you'll have the whole time it takes to slowly thaw from its icy prison to think about what you are going to buy with it (and whether you really need it). After the purchase has been made, put it back into a deep freeze so it won't tempt you.

However, if your credit card use really gets out of hand, the only surefire way to solve the problem is to put it out of its misery and cut it the hell up. If you are questioning whether or not you should do that, you already have your answer: Pick up the scissors.

Delinquency Strategy

What do you think of when you hear the word delinquent? Your friend who shoplifted candy bars? That guy who dated your sister in high school and drove a Camaro? The stoner cousin who spent time in juvenile detention? Well, delinquent has a whole new meaning now that you owe money to financial institutions. If you miss a scheduled payment, your loans will become delinquent. Don't panic, this sounds worse than it is. What exactly does it mean to be delinquent, and what are the consequences? The details will be different for every bank. Use financial self-advocacy, and call your loan servicer. Ask them about the specific penalties for missing a payment. As we've said before, it's better to know.

Let's say your loan payment is due on the 9th of every month, but for some reason you won't have enough money to pay it until you get that check from your day job on the 14th. Now, you plan to pay it as soon as you have the money, but from the 9th until the 14th your loans will be delinquent. You set panic aside, and you call your servicer. They tell you that delinquent loans don't even accrue any late fees until fifteen days after the loan becomes delinquent! Perfect. But just in case, how much are those late fees? Be sure to ask.

And what about your credit score? You ask your servicer when missed payments show up on your permanent credit history. They tell you thirty days. Brilliant. Now you have time to gather the money you owe and make that payment: fifteen days with no late fees, and thirty days before the missed payment shows up on your credit score. We call this the **delinquency strategy**: knowing the rules of loan delinquency and using their flexibility to your advantage.

Only use this strategy if absolutely necessary. If you use delinquency to give yourself more time to pay your loan, be aware that you will have less time the next month to gather the same amount of money and make the following payment. Can you get back on schedule by picking up another shift at your day job? Did you get a check from your grandmother for your birthday? Do your best to stay on schedule, and use the delinquency strategy only when needed. And remember: every financial institution will have different rules and policies, so be sure to use financial self-advocacy and call to ask for the information you need.

Credit Scores

Credit is not free money. In fact, using credit will almost certainly cost you more than paying for the same product with cash (your student loans should have taught you that by now). But realistically, you can't always pay for everything in cash. You will probably need to use credit to purchase a car, or to buy an apartment or house. Even if you rent an apartment, a landlord will look into your credit history before you sign the lease. You need to build up a good credit score to be approved. Do you know your credit score? Under the Fair Credit Reporting Act, you can get a free credit report from each credit bureau once a year. If you rotate between the three credit bureaus (TransUnion, Experian, and Equifax) you can get a free report every four months. Practice financial self-advocacy and make sure the information on your report is correct. Help protect yourself from identity theft and credit fraud.

Your credit report will show all the lines of credit you have ever opened and all the payments you have ever made. In addition, a credit report lists your current and past addresses, as well as the companies that have requested your credit history for commercial inquiries. Two types of credit inquiries exist: hard inquiries and soft inquiries. When a landlord checks your credit for a lease, or you apply for a mortgage or credit card, a hard inquiry occurs. A **hard credit inquiry** means that you give the lender or landlord the right to look at all of the information on your credit report, including your credit score. Based on the information they find, they decide whether or not to give you a loan, or lease you an apartment. A **soft credit inquiry** means that a person or company checks your score without asking for your permission, like when you get a letter saying you are pre-approved for a new credit card. A hard inquiry will actually lower your credit score a few points and remain on your credit report for two years. If you try to open up too many lines of credit, or try and sign too many leases, the large number of hard inquiries will begin to negatively affect your credit, which you should try to avoid. As for soft inquiries, you usually don't ask for them to occur, so they won't affect your credit score. Checking your own credit is considered a soft inquiry, and will not lower your score.

To get a free credit report, simply go to the website **annualcreditreport.com**, which is run by the three credit reporting bureaus: TransUnion, Experian, and Equifax. On the website you can choose which company to pull your report, but be careful, as each company will offer you unnecessary products that will cost you money, like negative credit monitoring and daily email notifications. Your free credit report doesn't come with a FICO score, but many credit card companies now offer it for free. A **FICO score** (short for Fair, Isaac, and Company) is a numerical measure of credit risk based on your credit report that ranges from 300 to 850. Keeping a good credit score is simple: make your payments on time (or within the allotted late payment schedule), check your credit report for free (three times a year), and use the power of financial self-advocacy to dispute any negative reporting or personal information that is incorrect. It's really that simple.

Health Care

How to Be a Healthy Artist

While you were in school, you probably had a health care plan through your university or stayed on your parents' insurance. Either way, you have had access to world-class health care, despite how annoying it may have been to wait at the university health center during one of those rare breaks in your curriculum. When you graduate, this will change. If you had a health care plan through your school, you will most likely have coverage until mid-August. If you have been on your parents' insurance, you might be able to stay on that plan a bit longer. A provision of the Affordable Care Act allows children to remain on a parent's insurance policy until the age of 26. If your parent is willing and able to do this for you, consider it as an option (and offer to help pay the premium). Regardless, the first thing you need to do is find out when your current health care ends. Again, do not procrastinate. Give yourself time to find new ways to access health care and secure health insurance. Many unions offer health insurance for their working members, though some just collectively bargain contracts and leave individuals to find health insurance on their own. How one qualifies for coverage can be confusing, but we'll try to explain the fine print for a selection of different unions. If you don't yet qualify for health insurance, or do not receive benefits through your union, we'll suggest other options for you at the end of the chapter.

Actors' Equity

Actors' Equity is the union for actors and stage managers in the theatre. Health insurance through Actors' Equity is based upon the number of weeks you have worked an Equity contract during the past year. You must have at least eleven weeks of employment in the previous year to qualify for six months of coverage. If you work nineteen or more weeks in the previous year, you will qualify for twelve months of coverage. Union members are evaluated for eligibility monthly. Now this may seem straightforward, but it gets complicated. We'll walk you through it.

The **accrual period** refers to a twelve-month period of time during which you have hopefully worked enough weeks to get coverage. The union will look back every month at the most recent accrual period (the last twelve months). If you are eligible for coverage, you then have a **waiting period**, which refers to the two-month gap between the accrual period and the benefit period. The **benefit period**, of course, refers to the months when you actually have coverage, which will be for six or twelve months. No matter how many times you read those last few sentences, it will seem confusing. Here is a concrete example to help explain how it works:

Let's say you finish acting school. Soon after graduation, you book a job out of town at a regional theater, which at long last gets you your Equity card. You have a luxurious contract that includes four weeks of rehearsal, a week of tech, and then a five-week run: an eternity by regional theater standards. Unfortunately, that only adds up to ten weeks of employment under an Equity contract, and you don't yet qualify for health insurance. You get back to New

York, and a non-profit like The Public Theater hires you for six weeks to understudy a play that just got extended. Life is good: you're working in New York and you now have enough weeks for health care. Equity looks back at the number of weeks you have worked in the past year (an accrual period) every month. In October, they look at the past year from October to the previous September, and you had ten weeks from your first job. You did not qualify for health care. But in November, they look at the next accrual period, the year from November back to the end of the previous October, and you will have an additional four weeks from the understudy job, for a total of fourteen weeks. You now qualify for six months of health care (You were five weeks shy of a full year of coverage, but your remaining weeks may count towards the next benefit cycle). However, you then have a waiting period of two months, so your coverage will officially start on January 1. This process repeats every month, with Equity reevaluating your qualifications.

Now the Equity system can be incredibly frustrating. Often you are only a week or two shy of health insurance at the end of a contract. In our example, you barely missed earning a full year of health care. You could wait and hope you get another job, thereby reaching the nineteen weeks necessary for the full year of coverage in the next quarter. We rarely recommend this however, because you never know when your next job will be. You have the possibility of losing weeks, if the next look back doesn't include the month where you earned unused benefit credit weeks.

What is Equity Health Care like? Equity offers medical and mental health through CIGNA Health Care and vision through Davis Vision. The quarterly premium for individuals in 2017 is only $100. However, coverage for dependents is much higher ($2,725.83 per quarter for a dependent, $4,414.27 for two or more dependents). *Equity does not include dental*, except through a separate self-pay program. Cigna offers a dental PPO (preferred provider organization) and a slightly cheaper dental HMO. For more information go to: www.equityleague.org/health.

Equity Health Care	
Weeks of Work Needed	11 weeks for 6 months 19 weeks for 12 months
Quarterly Premium for participant only	$100
Participant plus dependent	$2,725.83
Participant plus 2 or more dependents	$4,413.27

SAG-AFTRA

The Screen Actors Guild and the American Federation of Television and Radio Artists merged in 2012 and became a single union, SAG-AFTRA, which represents actors who work in radio, film, and television.

Health insurance through the SAG-AFTRA is based on earnings, or on a number of days worked on a union contract. Coverage is also separated into three tiers: one for people who made lots of money (Plan I), one for people who made somewhat less or meet the days worked requirement (Plan II), and one for people who have been in the union for ten years and made even less (Plan II Age and Service). We'll focus on the first two, since you probably have not been a member of SAG for ten years yet. You currently have to earn at least $17,000 or work 78 days to qualify for Plan II, and at least $33,000 for Plan I (as of early 2017). SAG-AFTRA looks back at your earnings not every month, but every three months (or quarter). Once you earn enough money on a union contract, however, your accrual period will remain the same as long as you meet the requirements for coverage, and coverage is always for an entire year. For SAG-AFTRA insurance, there is a three-month waiting period. The following rates for earnings requirements and premiums are for 2017:

SAG-AFTRA Health Care	Plan I	Plan II
Minimum earnings	$33,000	$17,000 or 78 days
Premium (per quarter) for participant only	$300	$357
Premium for participant plus dependent	$348	$408
Premium for participant plus 2 or more dependents	$375	$447

Let's say you are lucky enough to shoot a SAG-AFTRA commercial, it airs in February, and you make $20,000. The next look back is April 1. You qualify for a year of Plan II health insurance, and your accrual period is now April 1 - March 31, as long as you keep continual eligibility. After a three-month waiting period, your coverage will begin July 1.

Plan I includes medical, dental, and vision, while Plan II only includes medical and dental. SAG-AFTRA offers medical through the Industry Health Network and Blue Card PPO. Mental health is through Beacon Health Options, the dental plan is through Delta Dental, and vision is through Vision Service Plan. SAG-AFTRA is much better about dependents than Equity, with quarterly premiums rising only slightly for added dependents. For more detailed information about the health plans, go to the following SAG-AFTRA website: www.sagaftraplans.org.

IATSE

IATSE is the International Alliance of Theatrical Stage Employees, founded in 1893 by a group of stagehands. The union now includes local chapters that work together to represent quite an impressive assortment of artists and technicians: art directors, animators, costume designers, set designers, make-up artists, hair stylists, cinematographers, film editors, script supervisors, sound designers and technicians – and many, many others.

IATSE offers two different health insurance programs for its members, Plan A and Plan C. Individual locals may use one or both of these, or administer their own plans. Plan A is a traditional plan used by full-time or staff employees. Plan C is meant to address the needs of freelance workers. Both plans offer medical coverage through Empire Blue Cross and Blue Shield, dental benefits through Delta Dental or Self-Insured Dental Service (S.I.D.S.), and vision services through Davis Vision, and life insurance.

Plan A participants qualify once they have worked 60 days under a contract in a period of six consecutive months. Coverage begins on the first day of the second month after you complete the 60-day requirement, and continues for six months. If you work at least 60 days within the next six-month period, coverage will continue uninterrupted. Eligibility for Plan C coverage is a little more complicated. Union members must receive enough contributions made on their behalf by their employer into a CAPP Account (Contributions Available for Premium Payments). The contribution must equal the amount needed to pay one month's coverage under a version of Plan C called C-2 plus $150 administrative fee. A month's coverage is currently $774 in 2017, so the amount you need in your CAPP Account to qualify must equal $774 plus $150, so $924.

How are employer contributions calculated? Well, it varies based on the medium you are working in and the negotiated contract. Contracts may require a contribution that is a percentage of your fee, or a set amount per hour. An individual's CAPP Account grows as employers add welfare contributions. The contributions never expire, but continue to accrue over time until a member has enough money in their account to receive benefits.

For example, if you are a member of United Scenic Artists, IATSE Local 829, the 2016-2017 LORT contract currently requires a Welfare Fund employer contribution of 12% for theater designers and their assistants. If you design a play at a LORT B theater, scenery and costumes would currently make fees of $5,753, for a 12% contribution of $690.36. Assistant designers on the same LORT B contract would make $1,059 a week, for a contribution of $127.08 weekly. However, if you are a member of the Motion Picture Editors Guild, IATSE Local 700, the 2015-2018 Basic Agreement requires a producer to pay $4.113 into your account for each hour worked as a film editor.

IATSE offers a number of variations on Plan C that give different degrees and types of coverage at different rates. The plans are named C-1, C-2, C-3, C-4, and C-MRP. The smaller the number, the more comprehensive the coverage is, and the higher the premium. The C-MRP is a medical reimbursement plan available to members who have medical coverage from another source, like a spouse's employer or a teaching job. The National Benefit Fund deducts the cost of coverage from an individual's CAPP account each quarter. If there is not enough money to cover the cost, the individual must pay the difference.

IATSE Premiums	C-1	C-2	C-3	C-4
Individual	$5,325	$2,322	$1,506	$902
Family	$11,757	$4,131	$2,592	$1,737

AGMA

The American Guild of Musical Artists is a union that represents opera singers, dancers, opera directors, and - believe it or not - figure skaters. AGMA insurance falls into two categories: Plan A, which basically covers artists who are employed for an entire year or season, and Plan B, which covers artists who work freelance.

Plan A works like most traditional health insurance plans. You receive one month of health insurance for each month that a company pays the required contribution on your behalf. Basically, AGMA agreements require that employers make contributions to Plan A for artists on a weekly contract of four weeks or more, during which the artist works at least seven days in a four-week period. If you are contracted to work twenty weeks or more, a company must make the monthly Plan A health contributions for a full fifty-two weeks. Dependents may or may not be covered depending on the company. If it's your first time working for an AGMA employer, or you have had a break in work with an AGMA company, your insurance will begin two months after your contracted start date (and continue until two months after your employment has ended). AGMA offers health and dental through Aetna.

Changes in federal law brought about by the Affordable Care Act led AGMA to alter their other option, Plan B. The plan works like a health spending account, with employers contributing a percentage of earnings. The amount of the contribution varied based on the negotiated contract with different employers. Union members can now use that money to "buy-in" to Plan A coverage. In order to purchase Plan A coverage with funds from Plan B, members must have a minimum of $1200 in employer contributions or 32 weeks of covered employment. Find more information at: www.agmaretirement-health.org.

SDC

The Stage Directors and Choreographers Society is a union that (not so surprisingly) represents stage directors and choreographers. Union members are eligible for the health plan if they are employed on a SDC contract and their employer makes sufficient contributions to the SDC-League Health Fund on their behalf. If your employers contribute $1,200 during a six-month period, you will get 6 months of health care. If $2,400 accrues in that same period, you will receive a full year of paid benefits. If contributions are more than $1,200 but less than $2,400, the excess may be applied to the next period in order to meet the minimum eligibility level. In addition, your first rehearsal date(s) must fall within the corresponding six-month contribution period. The SDC uses look-back periods of January 1 - June 30 and July 1 - December 31.

Your benefit period will begin three months after the 6-month accrual period during which you qualify. The SDC has two different plan options.

Option A is a traditional insurance plan administered by Aetna Managed Choice in most of the country and Kaiser Permanente in California. The health fund will cover 85% of your premium, and you will have a **participant contribution** equal to the remaining 15% of the premium. You can include dependent children or your spouse on your plan, but must cover the entire cost of their premium.

Option B is a medical spending account offering $2,200 semiannually, or a $4,400 yearly maximum. This plan is not meant to replace basic health care, but is offered as a supplement for those already covered by another position or union (for example, an artistic director covered by a theater, a director already covered by another union like AEA or SAG, or a faculty member covered by a university). You can use Plan B to cover co-pays for other plans, or for additional expenses like dental, vision, or mental health. For more information, go to: www.sdcleaguefunds.org.

SDC Health Care	Option A	Option B
Employer contribution	$1,200 (6 months) $2,400 (12 months)	$1,200 (6 months) $2,400 (12 months)
Cost	15% of premium for individual, 100% of premium for family	No cost
Coverage	Traditional	Spending account $2,200 (6 months) $4,400 (12 months)

DGA

The Directors Guild of America represents film and television directors, as well as members of the directorial team: assistant directors, unit production managers, associate directors, stage managers and production associates. The DGA offers two tiers of health insurance, based on earnings. As of 2017, if you make $34,100-$105,999 in DGA covered employment, you qualify for coverage in the DGA Choice Plan. If you earn $106,000 or more, you qualify for the DGA Premier Choice Plan. The services provided by these two plans are the same if you use network providers. The difference is in non-network out-of-pocket limits and co-insurance.

The guild looks at your earnings every quarter to assess eligibility. After you meet the qualifications, there is a three-month wait before receiving benefits, which include health with Anthem Blue Cross, dental through Delta Dental, and vision with Vision Service Plan. There is no premium for participant-only coverage, a $780 annual fee to cover one dependent, and a $1,200 annual fee to cover your entire family. For more information, go to: www.dgaplans.org.

DGA Health Care	Choice	Premier Choice
Minimum earnings	$34,100	$106,000
Premium	$0	$0
Annual Dependent Fee	$780	$780
Two or More Dependents	$1,200	$1,200

Writers Guild

The Writers Guild of America represents writers of television and film, radio and new media. To qualify for health care, your employer must report your earnings to be at least equal to the WGA minimum for a one-hour network prime-time story and teleplay, which for 2015-2017 is $38,302. These earnings must be earned and reported during no more than four consecutive calendar quarters and, for eligibility purposes, will apply to the period in which the writing services are performed. After you have satisfied the earnings requirement, there is a three-month gap until coverage begins. Earnings cycles are divided into calendar quarters, so the union will look back for eligibility every three months. Dependent coverage includes your spouse and children as long as you pay the quarterly dependent premium of $150, which covers all dependents. The WGA offers health through Blue Cross Blue Card PPO and dental through Delta Dental. If you live in Southern California, you can reduce your costs further by receiving services through The Industry Health Network. Find out more at: www.wgaplans.org.

WGA Health Care	
Minimum earnings	$38,302
Premium	$0
Quarterly Dependent Premium	$150

Getting Insurance on Your Own

Qualifying for health insurance through your union can be a difficult process. Many art forms don't even have unions, or the unions don't provide options for health care. What can you do if you don't have health insurance? How do you find coverage on your own? The Affordable Care Act created state and national exchanges meant to encourage competition in the health insurance marketplace. At the same time, it mandated that all Americans have health insurance or face tax penalties. Basically, the hope is that large numbers of previously uninsured young (and therefore healthy) Americans will buy insurance and drive down the overall cost of plans. As an incentive, the government subsidizes premium costs for participants at lower income levels. Generally speaking, this should be good news for artists. The new health insurance marketplace is still in its infancy, and certainly has seen its share of problems (and publicity). However, it is definitely worth looking into: www.healthcare.gov.

Generic Prescriptions & $9 Birth Control

Regardless of your thoughts on the recent health care legislation, the endless news cycles did lend more exposure to the cost of reproductive health and the generic drug policies of major American retail stores. Target offers generic prescriptions (including birth control) for as little as $9 a month. Different retailers have different generic drug options and prices may vary by state, but the Target birth control plan can definitely help ease your budget.

Samuel J. Friedman Health Center

A partnership between The Actors Fund and Mount Sinai Doctors in New York City, the Samuel J. Friedman Health Center opened its doors on March 6, 2017. Located in

Times Square (in the same building as The Actors Fund) the Friedman Health Center provides health care to anyone working in the performing arts or entertainment industry. The Friedman Center replaces the Al Hirschfeld Free Health Clinic, which provided free health care for artists without health insurance. The Affordable Care Act led to a reduction in patients at the Hirschfeld, due to an increase in artists with insurance coverage. However, new challenges developed: high deductibles, narrow networks, and doctors not accepting certain insurance plans.

The Friedman offers primary and preventative care, as well as specialty care through the Mount Sinai Health System. Services are not free, but may be subsidized for those without insurance. The Actors Fund also provides health insurance counseling for the uninsured, helping artists enroll in plans available through state health insurance exchanges. For those who alternate between union plans and other types of insurance depending on employment and eligibility, the Friedman provides continuity of care by allowing you to stay with the same doctor.

To make an appointment, call 212.489.1939. The Friedman Health Center is located at 729 Seventh Avenue between 48th and 49th Streets in the heart of Time Square, easily accessible by public transportation. They do not accept walk-ins, so *you need to make an appointment in advance*. However, they do take same-day appointments if time slots are available. If you live in New York City, the Friedman Center is an invaluable resource, a health care provider specifically designed with artists in mind.

Unemployment

How Does It Work?

Because you have chosen to work in the arts as a profession, like it or not, you will probably be unemployed at some point. We all hope to move from job to job, finding consistent if not constant employment, but no matter how successful you are there may be lulls. When people not involved in the arts ask what being an artist is like, we tell them to imagine what it was like when they finished college and started interviewing for jobs. Unlike when they probably found full-time employment, the job of an artist will often last only for a day, a week, or a few months. When that job ends, the artist then starts an entire new round of job interviews. This cycle of short-term jobs followed by more job interviews continues indefinitely. That instability, and often a nomadic existence, is simply a way of life for many artists. Unemployment can help.

You may have grown up in a family where accepting help, especially from the government, is seen as a weakness. We're going to say this as unequivocally as we can: *There is absolutely no shame in collecting unemployment.* Employers support the system by paying payroll taxes on the earnings you make. As legislatures continue to cut arts funding in an attempt to balance unruly budget deficits, a subsidy that can help is unemployment. If it makes things easier, think of it as a grant to support your art, because that is what it will do. Don't get us wrong, it's not a terribly large amount of money, but it may help you through until your next job.

Every state in the union has slightly different qualifications and benefit rates. As newly minted artists fresh from training programs, we're going to take a stab in the dark and say that many of you will begin your artistic careers in New York or California. This is not to say that there aren't thriving artistic communities in other states (there are), but many of you will live and work in New York and California while figuring out if that's where you want to stay. To that end, we're going to cover the basics about unemployment insurance, and then specifics about the New York and California systems. Let's look at how it works.

The Basics About Unemployment

Simply put, you need to have worked in order to receive unemployment benefits. Employer payroll taxes support the unemployment system. States will look back at your most recent year of employment and determine your **benefit rate** (the amount of money you will receive each week) based on how much you have earned in the past year, or during a particular quarter of the past year. Your weekly benefit rate is determined by a mathematical equation that gives you a fraction of the earnings you made while employed. Each state sets that equation differently, which means that different states will have different benefit rates, even based on the same initial earnings. But basically, the more money you made before claiming unemployment, the more money you will receive in benefits.

You generally can't get unemployment if you were fired for misconduct or quit your job. However, there are numerous circumstances the government accepts as plausible reasons, one of which is that you lost your job due to "lack of work." Since unemployment for artists occurs when a show closes or a production wraps, this is considered lack of work, and you qualify.

In order to assess your qualifications for unemployment, the government will look back at your **base period,** which refers to a period of employment in covered work. Most states divide the year into four quarters, or three-month sections (January - March, April - June, July - September, and October - December). A **standard base period** refers to a twelve-month period consisting of the first four of the last five completed calendar quarters prior to a job loss. What the hell does that mean? It means that when the state looks back at your earnings, it won't initially include the most recent quarter. If you apply for unemployment after your first job out of school, your employment was probably in this most recent quarter, meaning you may be denied benefits at first. However, after this rejection you can reapply and ask for the state to use your alternative base period. An **alternative base period** refers to the amount a worker earned during the last four completed calendar quarters prior to a job loss. Using this base period, you may qualify, as it includes the most recent quarter of earnings.

A frustration for many artists is that the I-9 work of an independent contractor usually doesn't count toward unemployment. Since you are not technically an employee - you are your own employer - no one has paid unemployment payroll taxes on your behalf. Those taxes pay for unemployment, so I-9 wages will generally not qualify you for benefits.

You can't live on unemployment for very long, and that is intentional. The benefit rates are meant to support you while you look for work, not to replace work. Your benefit rate will most likely only cover the bare minimum of expenses in your budget. The strategy that will make it helpful is to save money when you do have artistic work, find additional part-time or freelance work that will supplement unemployment, or only use it briefly until you find a subsistence job.

After you file you will be sent a **monetary determination**, which should show your base period and the employers and wages used to determine if you had sufficient employment to establish a claim. The first time you file, it would be at this point that you might get a rejection notice, and have to request that the government use your alternate base period, although some states will do this automatically. If you received notification by mail the form to reapply should be included, though you can also download it online. You need to return your re-application form promptly after receiving your monetary determination. We understand this might be frustrating and confusing.

Once you have a valid claim and benefit rate, you must request payment by claiming benefits each week. Before you receive any benefits, however, most states have an **unpaid waiting period** of one full week. So the first time you certify benefits for a new claim, you will be requesting credit for your waiting week. For each following week that you are unemployed, you will request payment at the end of that week, probably on Sunday. You can claim benefits online, over the phone, or by regular mail, though we recommend doing it online. When you claim your benefits, you'll probably have to answer a series of questions certifying that you were ready, willing, and able to work during the past week. If you sign up for direct deposit, which is the easiest way to receive your benefits, it will be deposited to your account within a few days.

Your claim period lasts for one year, which is called your benefit period. Most states allow you to receive only 26 times your full weekly rate during the benefit period, meaning you can collect state benefits for half of the weeks in that year. However, once you have exhausted state benefits, you may qualify for an extension through certain federal jobless benefits. **Emergency unemployment compensation** and **extended benefits** will each lengthen the amount of time you can receive benefits. During times of economic crisis, the federal government often extends these policies in an attempt to help the chronically unemployed. Realistically, however, you will likely need a subsistence job in non-artistic field to pay your bills long before your reach extended benefits.

Hopefully unemployment will allow you a few weeks or months to get back on your feet and find artistic work, or time to find that subsistence job. If you do get another job during the year of your claim, and that job ends before your benefit period does, your claim will still be open. This means that you won't have to re-file: just start claiming benefits again online. You will have to verify your most recent employer, but you won't have a waiting period again.

You should apply for unemployment during your first week of total or partial unemployment. We would definitely suggest doing so online, since the process over the phone is frustrating. Know that whenever you call unemployment, you will probably be on hold for a very long time before speaking to anyone. This may fluctuate, but depending on the current economy and the number of people filing for unemployment, the Department of Labor can often get overwhelmed. Even if you apply online, you probably will have to call toward the end and talk to someone on the phone, but you'll receive instructions about that during the online application process. You will most likely need the following information:

1. Your Social Security number.

2. A valid Driver's License or Non-Driver Photo Identification Card number.

3. Employer Registration number or Federal Employer Identification Number of your most recent employer (you may need to email someone in human resources for this number).

4. Name, address, zip code and phone number of your most recent employer.

5. If you are choosing to have direct deposit of your weekly benefits (which we would recommend), you'll need a check handy in order to enter your bank routing and checking account numbers.

Now let's look at the plans of New York and California.

New York

File a claim at **www.labor.ny.gov** at any time, or by calling the Telephone Claims Center at 1-888-209-8124 from 8 am to 5 pm, Monday through Friday. In New York, here are the requirements to qualify for unemployment:

1. You must have worked and have been paid wages for employment in at least two calendar quarters in your base period.

2. You must have been paid at least \$2,100 in wages in one of the calendar quarters in your base period (as of 2017).

3. The total wages paid to you in your base period must be at least one and one-half times your high quarter wages. If your high-quarter earnings are equal to or great than \$9,460, your wages in the other base period quarters must total at least half that number, or \$4,730.

Your benefit rate is then generally set as 1/26 or 1/25 of the high-quarter wages paid to you in your base period (depending on your income level). If you only have earnings in two or three quarters of the year, your benefit rate is calculated from an average of the two highest quarters instead of just the highest quarter. The maximum weekly rate you can currently receive is \$430, and the minimum rate is \$100. What exactly does that all mean? Let's look at a New York example.

Since you have been in undergraduate or graduate school for the last two to four years, you have more than likely not been able to hold down a job. When you finish school, you will therefore have a base period (the year long look back at your earnings) with cumulative earnings of \$0. You have not been employed in the last year, so even though you are now currently unemployed, you do not qualify. If by some chance you've been able to work part time, you may qualify, but your benefit rate will probably be quite small.

For the sake of example, let's say that you're an actor, you give a great audition for the Public Theater, and they cast you in the non-Equity (non-union) ensemble for the first Shakespeare play in Central Park. The contract is for ten weeks: four weeks of rehearsal and a six-week run. You make $400 a week, and the show closes at the very end of June. You think to yourself, "Well maybe I can go on unemployment, and use that to support myself while I audition." When the government looks back at the last year of your earnings (your base period), you have made $4,000, but only in one quarter (April-June). You have not been paid wages in at least two calendar quarters of your base period. You do not yet qualify for unemployment.

About a month later, however, you get your first regional theater job. Rehearsals began in early August and the contract lasts for ten weeks, with the run ending in late October. You make $800 a week. You think to yourself, "well now I should be able to go on unemployment." The government looks at the four quarters of the prior year, your base period. The first two quarters you were in school and made $0. The third quarter you made $4,000 doing Shakespeare in the Park. For the fourth quarter (the most recent quarter, July - September), you were unemployed in July but made $800 a week for three weeks of August and all four weeks of September. You have earnings of $5,600. You now have earnings in consecutive quarters, the first requirement. You have also been paid at least $2,100 in one of those quarters, the second requirement. The third requirement is the confusing one. The total wages paid to you in your base period ($4,000 + $5,600 = $9,600) must be 1.5 times your highest quarter wages. Your highest quarter wages are $5,600, 1.5 x $5,600 = $8,400. Your total wages for the last year were $9,600, which was more than $8,400. You qualify for unemployment!

The maximum amount you can receive in New York State is $430 per week. So looking at our example, you made $0 in the first quarter, $0 in the second quarter, $4,000 in the third quarter, and $5,600 in the fourth quarter. Since you did not have earnings in all four quarters, your benefit rate will be calculated from an average of your two highest earnings quarters. The average of $4,000 and $5,600 is $4,800. 1/26 of $4,800 is $184.62. Now you may think to yourself, that is not very much money. You'd be right. You can't live on $738.46 a month. However, collecting unemployment may allow you a little breathing room before your next job, or before you find supplemental work to help you through to your next artistic endeavor.

Just for fun, let's work through one more example. As a theater actor, the most lucrative contract around (again, not including television or film) is a Broadway production contract. Let's say you have a spectacular audition, you land a Broadway show, and that Broadway show is a hit. You run for a year, and the contract is a production contract (not a LORT contract like you might get at Roundabout or Lincoln Center). Minimum salary in 2017 is $1,974 a week, and you have that salary for the entire high quarter of your base period, meaning your earnings will be $25,662 for that three-month period. Your benefit rate, if calculated as 1/26 of $25,622 would be $987. Unfortunately, unemployment is capped at $430 a week in New York. Your benefit rate in this example, then, is $430, meaning your monthly budget is $1,720. You can *almost* live on that, but it still points out that you better be saving some of your Broadway paycheck.

There is also a way to combat the problem we found in our first example, the fact that you were not working every week of your high-earnings quarter. You can file a form called the "Request for Rate Based on Weeks of Unemployment" that will recalculate your rate based on your weekly salary. You must provide proof, such as paycheck stubs, for each week of work. You must have at least 20 weeks of work in your base period. *Your benefit rate would then be calculated as one half your average weekly wage* (1/2 x total base period wages/total weeks worked). In our example you made $800 a week for the seven weeks of your contract that fell in your high-earnings quarter. Using the standard calculations, you would get $184.62. However, using the weekly rate you would look at all your earnings for the base year. You rate would then be 1/2 x $9,600/17, and you would get a payment of $282.35. This is definitely something you should consider, as it increases your benefits by $100 a week. Again, you must fill out this form within 10 days of receiving your monetary determination.

"What if I work part time to supplement my benefits?" you ask. If you work less than four days in a week, and make less than $430, you can still claim benefits but you will receive only a partial amount. Each day or part of a day of work will result in a payment of a partial benefit as follows: 1 day of work = 3/4 of your full rate, 2 days of work = 1/2 of your full rate, 3 days of work = 1/4 of your full rate, 4 days of work = no benefits due. If you work while receiving benefits and do not report that employment, even if it is part-time work, you could be committing fraud. Unfortunately, this includes freelance work and self-employment. Know that it is dangerous to bend or break these rules, and could ultimately result in a suspension of your benefits and criminal charges.

California

File a claim at **www.edd.ca.gov** or call 1-866-333-4606 to use the Automated Self-Service telephone system, twenty-four hours a day, seven days a week.

In order to assess your qualifications for unemployment, the California EDD (Employment Development Department) will look back at your base period using the same calendar as New York State. Again, the most recent earnings quarter will not initially be included. All of the terms used in the California State section mean the same thing so if you get lost, refer back to the beginning of the chapter, or check the glossary. Here are the requirements you need to qualify in California, the main difference from New York being you only need one of these requirements:

1. Have earned at least $1,300 in the highest quarter of the base period (as of late 2015).

2. Have earned at least $900 in the highest quarter AND earned total base period earnings of at least 1.25 times the high quarter earnings. For example, if you have $900 earnings in the highest quarter, you are required to have earned a total of $1,125 in the base period ($900 x 1.25 = $1,125).

Your benefit rate is then set as 1/26 of the high quarter wages paid to you in your base period. The maximum weekly rate you can receive is $450, and the minimum is $40. What exactly does all this mean? Let's take a look at an example of unemployment in California:

As a young filmmaker who just graduated from USC, you land a job as a production assistant. You take coffee orders, make contacts, and work on a film that will get an extended theatrical release. You make $100 a day for a shoot lasting thirty days, so $3,000 over the length of the production during the months of June and July. The production ends through no fault of your own, and you apply for unemployment. When you apply on September 1st, California looks back at your **standard base period** (which is the first four of the last five completed calendar quarters prior to the date you file your claim), which turns out to be April of your junior year through March of your senior year. However, because you were in school and not earning any money during your standard base period, you made $0 and you do not qualify for unemployment.

Next, because you don't qualify under the standard base period, California automatically looks back at your alternate base period, which consists of the last four completed calendar quarters prior to the date you file your claim. This means the state is now looking back over your earnings from July during the summer between your junior and senior year to this past June when you started your PA job. They see that in June you had a total of $1000 in earnings from the first ten days of shooting, which is again not enough to reach either of the earnings requirements, and you still do not qualify for unemployment.

So you keep at it, and keep landing gigs throughout the year: a few more PA jobs, a restaurant job, and some freelance editing work. You make around $6,000 a quarter, and when you finish another PA job the following June, you realize you've already been out of film school for a year. You apply for unemployment again, and because you have earned at least $1,300 in the highest quarter of your base period, you finally qualify for unemployment!

California uses a similar method for finding your benefit rate as New York, calculated as 1/26 of your highest earnings quarter. If your highest earnings quarter was $6,000, divide that by 26 and you have a benefit rate of $230.76. However, California rounds up, so you will receive a weekly payment of $231. Your claim is open for one year, during which you can claim benefits for 26 weeks. Now $231 a week means a budget of $924 a month, which is not very much money. But it may help you survive until you start another support job, or begin working full time as an AD for that director you met last summer when you got her coffee working as a PA.

According to California, while on unemployment you must be actively looking for work through the EDD, your union, or on your own every week to qualify for your weekly benefits. While the strictness and frequency of the state checking on this requirement may vary, it is still a good idea to actually be looking for work every week and keeping the records that you are. So, if you're an actor or director with an agent, keep records of all the auditions and meetings that they get for you. If you're an animator or designer, keep records of all the resumes you send. If you don't have an agent, or are not in a union, register with EDD Workforce Services, and keep records of all the job searches you do through their databases.

Like New York, if you're working part-time, California requires you report that fact when you claim your weekly benefits. However, California bases the reduction of your weekly benefit rate due to part-time work solely on earnings. "If your weekly earnings are $100 or less, the first $25 dollars does not count. The amount of earnings more than $25 is subtracted from your weekly benefit amount and you are paid the difference, if any" and "if your weekly earnings are $101 or more, the first 25 percent does not count. The amount of earnings remaining is subtracted from your weekly benefit amount and you are paid the difference, if any." Please note that earnings of any kind, including things like jury duty and residual pay (from all those TV gigs you did last year), must be reported to the EDD. Failure to do so may affect your ability to claim weekly benefits and result in criminal charges. Also, California State unemployment is based on how many days you are able to work, so if you are sick for a few days and unable to accept work offers, you must claim that as well or your ability to claim weekly benefits may also be affected, or result in criminal charges.

There are three ways to certify your weekly benefits in California: by mail, by telephone, or online. You can certify your claim by telephone using the EDD Tele-Cert system (1-866-333-4606). It is fully automated, available twenty-four hours a day, and is a useful option if you find yourself without Internet access. The best option, however, is using the online claim certification system, the EDD Web-Cert: **www.edd.ca.gov**. You can do this anywhere you have access to the Internet, making it the easiest method.

Unemployment Insurance in California issues payment through an EDD Debit Card. The EDD Debit Card is a Visa debit card administered by Bank of America, onto which your weekly benefits will be deposited. You can request a transfer of your weekly benefits to your checking account or set up direct deposit. You must contact Bank of America to make either of these changes. Regardless, the initial payment will arrive as an EDD Debit Card.

What Else Should I Know?

Another suggestion we will make is about taxes. Your unemployment benefits are taxable, and will be counted as income on your next tax return. You should have the option of having a percentage of your benefits withheld for taxes, and we would recommend doing that.

Finally, know that claiming unemployment is sometimes a bureaucratic nightmare. If you worked a job outside of the state where you live (and artists often travel) you may have to wait for the state where you worked to report your earnings to the state where you live. They may not show up automatically, and you and the Department of Labor of your home state may have to request those earnings. Any number of other problems may hold up the proceedings, and this can be intensely frustrating, especially if you were counting on that money. No matter how frustrated you get though, keep claiming benefits. When everything is finally sorted out, the state will release payment for all of those weeks and you will belatedly get a lump sum directly deposited into your checking account.

Unemployment won't sustain you forever, but it can be an incredibly helpful support system. Take advantage of what it has to offer, consider it a grant that supports your art, and try not to get frustrated or overwhelmed. That next job is just around the corner.

Tips and Tricks

Ways to be Thrifty and Proactive

What you will find in the following section is a list of ideas that can help your budget and your heart - some practical, some frivolous. We hope that you'll add to this list, sharing these ideas and others with your fellow artists, making your life and budget a little less stressful. Welcome to the lighter side of finance. Being thrifty isn't simply about cutting coupons. Go ahead and use your imagination, and by all means, have some fun!

Financial

Credit Unions. Credit unions are non-profit banks whose main goal is to serve their members, not to maximize profits. The two most well known credit unions for artists are the Actors Federal Credit Union (based in NYC) and the First Entertainment Credit Union (based in LA). As their names would suggest, the AFCU and FECU are very artist-friendly, offering accounts without fees, low-interest loans, low-interest credit cards, retirement accounts, and free in-network ATM use (in New York that includes every McDonald's location, and in LA at 7-Elevens). You don't have to be an actor or performer to join, as these banks accept members from across the spectrum of artistic disciplines and unions. If you don't yet qualify for membership in the AFCU or FECU, there are many other credit unions that may help. For example, city employees, teachers, and the military all have credit unions. Most accept family members of a qualified applicant as well (if you don't qualify, it's possible a family member or spouse does). For more details go to: **www.actorsfcu.com** and **www.firstent.org**.

Citibank MasterCard. You can pay off your student loan debt using credit card rewards points. Yes, you read that correctly. The rewards program at Citibank MasterCard is called "Thank You" and you can sign up online at www.thankyou.com. Every dollar spent earns points, and those rewards points can eventually buy a student loan rebate check. 2,500 points gets you $25.00, and 10,000 points gets you $100.00. You don't have to have student loans with Citibank to qualify either. Customers can apply their points toward any student loan program or financial institution. Call to redeem your points and Citibank will make the check out to your loan servicer (for example, if you do have loans through Citibank, the check is made out to their servicer: the Student Loan Corporation). Citibank mails the rebate check to you, and you send it on to the servicer. If you want the check to go to a specific loan (one with a higher interest rate perhaps), include the exact loan number on the check. For Citibank loans, the address is: Student Loan Corporation, c/o Citibank, 8725 W. Sahara Avenue, Attn: Exception Payments, Mail Zone 1225, Las Vegas, NV 89117.

Be Kind to Yourself

Collective Coupons. Blending communism and capitalism, the phenomenon of collective coupons offers deals on restaurants, bars, movie theaters, spas, and vacations. How does it work? A business offers a deal, usually at a steep discount (and often as much as 50%). If a certain number of people buy the deal, everyone gets it. If not enough people buy it, no one gets it. A lot of different companies are getting in on the act. Start looking for deals at the following sites: Groupon, LivingSocial, Gilt City, Google Offers, and Thrillist.

Sample Sales. Ever have the urge to buy a new wardrobe but don't want your budget to explode? If you live in New York or Los Angeles, you reside in one of the world capitals of fashion. Take advantage of this by embracing two simple words: sample sale. At a sample sale, a designer or label sells unwanted merchandise at astonishingly low prices. They unload products from the previous season, clothes used in photo shoots, pieces that never made it into stores, and labels that never took off. Sample sales are usually unpublicized, and last anywhere from a few hours to couple of weeks. Often they are in odd and temporary places. Some require an RSVP or an entrance fee, but the clothes you can find and the prices you will pay are well worth the hassle. Sample sale boutiques may temporarily pop up in fashion districts, and they are rapidly moving online. Start your search for Internet sample sales at these sites: The Choosy Beggar, Gilt, and The Stylish City.

MAC Cosmetics. Need new makeup? Have no fear! Performers of any entertainment union can join the MAC Pro Membership Program. For a $35 annual fee, you are entitled to 30% off MAC Cosmetics (40% off if you're a makeup artist), classes, events, and free shipping on orders over $100. Get your pretty on at www.maccosmetics.com.

Alumni Status

Student IDs. Hang on to those Student IDs. If you look closely at the expiration date, it may be active for at least another year. As you may know, many arts and entertainment organizations offer discounted tickets to students. For example, you can still take advantage of discounts at museums, galleries, opera, theater, and dance. Now that you finally have time to have a life, get one. Take advantage of your Student ID, and use it!

Stay Healthy

Alumni Gym Memberships. Your alma mater probably offers a discount to alumni for membership at their campus gyms. If you still live nearby, you can get access to all of the athletic facilities for a fraction of the cost.

Yoga. Is your root chakra tied up in knots because you can't afford yoga class? Look for studios with suggested donations, like Yoga to the People. Or sign up for Yogaglo, an online service that streams unlimited classes for a variety of skill levels and styles. A subscription costs $18 a month and you can take as many classes as you want. Om!

P90X. Cancel your gym membership and get ripped at home with this DVD workout system. Start cross training with Tony Horton at www.beachbody.com/p90x.

Fitness Blender. Need a workout that's completely free? Choose from over five hundred different workout videos for every fitness level at www.fitnessblender.com.

Union Discounts

Union membership does have its perks, and many discounts are tailored to specific disciplines. After you join your union, log into the website and scan the membership section for what could be of use. You'll find things like discounts on tickets, local businesses, restaurants, insurance, travel, rental cars, and financial services. Another great resource is Union Plus, which provides discounts and services for members of any union, from Actors' Equity to the UAW.

AT&T Union Discount. As the only unionized wireless service, AT&T offers a 15% discount on all coverage with membership in any union. This one is a no-brainer. Find out more at the Union Plus website.

Volunteer Income Tax Assistance. In addition to discounts, many unions offer a free income tax prep service called the Volunteer Income Tax Assistance program. With VITA you get the free help of a trained volunteer with a savvy mind for artist taxes. But don't wait to the last minute. You might find yourself in a line outside on a snowy morning at 5 am, like many actors do at the New York offices of Actors Equity. Look for the details and schedule of VITA services on the website of your union. If you have yet to join a union, or your union doesn't provide VITA, local or city governments often offer similar services. Go to the IRS website for help locating the VITA center nearest you.

The Actors Fund. The Actors Fund is a nonprofit organization serving all entertainment professionals. A truly remarkable resource, their services include assistance with mental health, chemical dependency, HIV/AIDS, affordable housing, financial emergencies, career counseling and job training. The Samuel J. Friedman Health Center and the Phyllis Newman Women's Health Initiative address urgent health care needs. The Dancers' Resource creates a support system for professional dancers, and the Financial Wellness Program offers seminars about money and debt. Not all programs require union membership, but some will. Go to www.actorsfund.org to find out more information. Take advantage of their help when you need it, and then donate money if and when you can. Why do we love the Actors Fund? Consider the simplicity and generosity of this obscure program: in 1945, NYC actor Conrad Cantzen bequeathed his estate to the Actors Fund, asking them to buy shoes for future generations of actors. He wanted them to walk confidently into auditions, not "down at the heels." He knew what it was like, and he wanted to help. Buy a pair of shoes for less than $100, and get reimbursed for $40. The eligibility requirements include current unemployment in your entertainment field, paid-up union membership, and no prior application to the Conrad Cantzen Shoe Fund in the last 24 months.

Artists Financial Support Group

The **Artists Financial Support Group** was founded in the fall of 2010 by alumni of the NYU Graduate Acting Program. After finishing an elite artistic training program, we found ourselves working in the arts, and yet still struggling with debt and student loans. We began to realize that we might not be able to afford to be artists, simply because we had gone to school to be artists. Leaving shame and panic aside, we decided to focus instead on working toward positive change. We now invite you to become a part of our growing community. Know that you're not alone, and that together we can make a difference.

How can you do that? Join our mailing list. Like us on Facebook and follow us on Twitter. Download the podcasts from our website. But most importantly, talk to your classmates and peers about your debt, and share ideas and information. Become politically active. Use financial self-advocacy. And if you have questions, ask. The AFSG is both a resource and a community of which you are now a part. Check out our website at:

www.artistsfinancial.org

Finally, at the beginning of the book we offered a brief disclaimer, stating that the members of the AFSG are artists, not financial planners, and that you should use self-advocacy to learn about your specific situation and make informed choices. With this in mind, here is a more formal legal statement of that disclaimer:

NOTICE: The information in this book is intended to be for educational purposes only. We are not professional advisors and we encourage you to seek out advice when necessary. The information contained in this book may change from state to state, and is intended to be updated periodically. We are not endorsing any product or service referred to in this guide. Finally, we cannot guarantee the outcome of any action that may be recommended.

The simple act of buying and reading this book means that you are well on your way to financial self-advocacy. Student loans create a significant burden on the lives of artists, but it is possible to take control of your financial life. Remember that you are not alone, and know that with perseverance your student loans can and will be repaid.

Glossary

Simple Definitions to Financial Terms

accrual period: the period of time used to determine whether you have met the requirements to get health insurance from your union.

The Actors Fund: a remarkable nonprofit organization serving all entertainment professionals. The services they provide include assistance with mental health, chemical dependency, HIV/AIDS, health care, affordable housing, financial emergencies, financial wellness, career counseling and job training.

adjustable interest rate: a percentage-based bank fee that fluctuates over time, usually expressed as a percentage above the prime rate.

adjusted gross income (AGI): the money you make in a year, minus the deductions you claim on your tax return. Used to calculate payments on the PAYE, IBR, and ICR student loan repayment plans.

alternative base period: the amount a worker earned during the last four completed calendar quarters prior to a job loss. A worker may request that the government use this instead of the standard base period to calculate unemployment.

amortization: paying off a loan. The word comes from the Latin "mort," meaning death. So basically, think of it this way: you are slowly killing your loan.

annual percentage rate (APR): an interest rate charged by a bank that is calculated annually. The bank charges this percentage of your loan each year as a fee for taking out the loan; it's how they make money.

Artists Financial Support Group (AFSG): a non-profit organization (founded and run by artists) that seeks to educate student and professional artists about financial self-advocacy, advocate for legislative and institutional change in the cost of arts education, and innovate new ways to manage student loan debt and to budget on an erratic income. We also wrote this book.

base period: a yearlong period of time used to determine unemployment benefits.

benefit period: 1. the months when you have health coverage. 2. the 12 months in which your unemployment claim is valid, during which you may only receive 26 times your benefit rate.

benefit rate: the amount of money you will receive each week on unemployment.

budget: an estimate of income and expenses for a set period of time.

capitalization: when unpaid interest is folded into the base amount of your loan, causing the loan to increase in size.

collective coupon: a deal offered by a business, usually at a steep discount (often as much as 50%). If a certain number of people buy the deal, everyone gets it. If not enough people buy it, no one gets it.

consolidation: combining smaller loans with differing interest rates into one larger loan with a single interest rate.

credit union: a nonprofit financial cooperative (similar to a bank) whose main goal is to serve their members, not to maximize profits.

deferment: a period of time in which repayment is postponed temporarily for specific situations, such as economic hardship or unemployment, or enrollment in school. Any interest accruing on subsidized loans will be paid by the government.

default: failure to meet financial obligations.

delinquency strategy: knowing the rules of loan delinquency and using their flexibility to your advantage.

discretionary income: the amount of money you have left to spend after paying for essentials like food, clothing, and shelter. The different income-based repayment options for student loans calculate this amount differently.

extended repayment: a federal loan-repayment plan in which you will pay a fixed amount each month until your loans are paid in full over a period not to exceed 25 years. You may want to choose this option if you have a manageable amount of debt.

federal loans: loans offered to you by the government at reduced interest rates, for which they guarantee repayment to the lender.

FICO score: a numerical measure of credit risk based on your credit report that ranges from 300 to 850.

financial self-advocacy: the assertion of self-determination and personal responsibility in your financial life (you only get what you ask for).

fixed interest rate: a percentage-based bank fee that remains the same throughout the life of a loan.

forbearance: a temporary postponement or reduction of payments for a period of time because the borrower experiences financial difficulty. Unlike deferment, none of the interest accruing on your loans will be paid by the government during forbearance. You don't want to go into forbearance unless you have already exhausted your deferments.

grace period: an optional period of time at the beginning of repayment during which the lender does not require payment from the borrower. We strongly suggest you consider this time as a *prepare period*.

graduated repayment: a loan-repayment plan in which monthly payments start out low and increase every two years. The length of the repayment period can be either standard (10 years) or extended (25 years). This plan is generally for people who expect their income to increase steadily over time, which is not necessarily true for artists. We don't recommend this option for federal loans, but it might be necessary if you don't have other options for your private loans.

hard credit inquiry: when a lender or landlord gets your permission to look at all of the information on your credit report, including your credit score.

income-based repayment (IBR): a federal loan-repayment plan which bases your monthly payments on your income, a new and improved version of the ICR.

income-contingent repayment (ICR): a federal loan-repayment plan which bases your monthly payments on your income, an older and inferior version of the IBR.

interest rate: the fee a bank charges you for borrowing money, calculated as a percentage of the original loan amount. The fee is calculated annually, and therefore is often referred to as an annual percentage rate.

lender: the bank that initially loaned you money, or that later bought your loan.

monetary determination: an unemployment insurance document that lists your base period, summarizes the employers and wages used to establish a claim, and sets your benefit rate.

negative amortization: a situation in which your loan payment does not cover the amount of interest you owe on a loan. If that interest is capitalized (added to the principal, or initial amount) at the end of the year, the size of your loan will increase even though you are making payments every month.

origination fee: an activation fee, a charge incurred for beginning a transaction with a bank. Think of it like a handling fee from Ticketmaster but a lot more money. Calculated as a percentage of the original loan.

partial financial hardship: a requirement for the PAYE and IBR plans, it really just means that your monthly payment on these plans would be less than on standard repayment.

participant contribution: for SDC union members, the cost of health care, an amount equal to 15% of the insurance premium.

Pay As You Earn (PAYE): a federal loan-repayment plan that bases your monthly payments on your income, a new and improved version of the IBR. We recommend this option especially for graduate students, since the term of the loan (and path to forgiveness) is only 20 years.

Perkins Loan: a subsidized federal loan given to students with exceptional financial need.

PLUS Loan: federal loans available to the parents of undergraduates, as well as to graduate or professional degree students. They help defray additional educational expenses not covered by other options. The amount you can borrow is the cost of attendance (determined by the individual school) minus any other financial assistance received. Graduate PLUS Loans can be consolidated with other federal loans; Parent PLUS Loans cannot.

poverty level: minimum level of income necessary for an adequate standard of living, as determined by the government. Used to calculate monthly payments on the PAYE, IBR and ICR.

prime rate: the interest rate set by banks for loans given to the most credit worthy borrowers; used as the reference point for adjustable interest rates (and varies).

principal: the base amount of the loan.

private loans: loans not guaranteed or subsidized by the government and offered by private lenders, which are probably not as advantageous in terms of interest rates and repayment plans. They cannot be consolidated with your government loans.

reverse budget: a financial plan in which you monitor your expenses in order to determine how much money you need to make each month.

Revised Pay As You Earn (REPAYE): a federal loan-repayment plan that bases your monthly payments on your income, a new and mostly improved version of PAYE. We recommend this option for many borrowers because its interest subsidy slows the effect of negative amortization.

sample sale: a sale at which a designer or label sells unwanted merchandise at astonishingly low prices.

servicer: the organization that sends you loan statements and bills on behalf of the lender.

soft credit inquiry: when a company looks at your credit history without your permission in order to offer you more lines of credit.

Samuel J. Friedman Health Center: a medical clinic for artists in Times Square, a partnership between The Actors Fund and Mount Sinai Doctors in New York City.

Stafford Loan: a loan offered to students that is guaranteed by the government, allowing students to borrow at lower interest rates. The loan can be subsidized or unsubsidized.

standard base period: the 12-month period consisting of the first four of the last five completed calendar quarters prior to a worker's job loss. Basically, that means that when the government looks back at your earnings for Unemployment Benefit purposes, it won't initially include the most recent quarter.

standard repayment: a federal loan repayment plan in which you will pay a fixed amount each month until your loans are paid in full over a period of 10 years. You may want to choose this option if you have a small amount of student debt.

sticker shock: the moment when you open a loan statement envelope and see exactly how much you owe, as opposed to what you thought you owed.

subsidized loan: a loan for which the government will pay the interest accruing while the student is in college, during the grace period, and during deferment.

unpaid waiting period: the first week after claiming unemployment, during which one does not receive a benefit check.

unsubsidized loan: a loan for which the government does not pay the interest while the student is in college, during the grace period, or during deferment.

Volunteer Income Tax Assistance (VITA): free income tax preparation assistance; often run by unions or local governments.

waiting period: a three-month gap between the time you qualify for health insurance and your benefit period begins.

Made in the USA
Middletown, DE
25 February 2020

85319325R00066